D1556553

RAILWAY HERALDRY
and other insignia

RAILWAY HERALDRY
and other insignia

by

GEORGE DOW
FRSA FCIT

DAVID AND CHARLES

ISBN o 7153 5896 o

Printed in Great Britain at The Pitman Press Bath Somerset
for David & Charles (Holdings) Limited Newton Abbot Devon

Contents

*To the memory of
my mother and father
for their love and wisdom*

Armorial Devices in Colour

BLACK AND WHITE ILLUSTRATIONS appear throughout the book, and are identified in bold type in the Index, see page 261.

8

Introduction

No product of the Industrial Age was more colourful than the British steam hauled passenger train of the period extending from late Victorian to early Georgian days.

Each railway company—and there were more than a hundred of them—indulged in distinctive liveries for its locomotives and coaching stock which, with the then cheap and plentiful labour, were generally kept in immaculate condition. The colours employed ranged from various shades of green, blue, red, brown and yellow to black for the engines and to teak or mahogany finish for the coaches. Boiler bands and side panels of the engines and window, door and waist panels of the coaches were almost invariably lined-out, occasionally rather extravagantly, in contrasting colours. Lettering and numbering, usually in gilt characters, were often elaborately shaded. Brass door handles and grab rails, sometimes preceded by brass dome and safety valve covers, would glisten like gold. The final touch, in many cases, would be the company's armorial device, colourful and occasionally ornate, dignified and utterly appropriate, emblazoned on locomotives and coaches alike.

Add to this cavalcade of colour the ingredients which brought it all to life . . . the plume of smoke, the wisps of steam, the whiff of hot oil and the unforgettable euphony of steam power being transformed to movement through steel wheels upon steel rails, and there was created a picture the like of which we shall never see again.

The existence of a railway company began with the granting of the Royal Assent to its Act of Incorporation, when the seal was at once brought into use for the completion of legal documents. The design of the seal embraced, more often than not, the arms or parts of the arms of the principal towns served by the line. And from the seal stemmed the armorial device which became the public insignia of many British railways from the earliest times.

Surprisingly, the design of the armorial device did not originate in the College of Arms, although in at least one instance, and doubtless there were others, the advice of somebody at the College of Arms was sought over the design of a seal. The known case is that of the nascent Manchester, Sheffield & Lincolnshire Railway, the future Board of which, in the autumn of 1846, requested the Lancaster Herald to furnish a design for the seal. This appreciation of matters heraldic by the Manchester, Sheffield & Lincolnshire was manifested by its successors, the Great Central and the London & North Eastern, which, almost alone amongst British railway companies, obtained grants of armorial bearings. The Southern Railway, the British Transport Commission and the Ulster Transport Authority were the only other undertakings to do so.

The earliest railway armorial devices were most frequently to be seen on passenger coaches, uniform buttons and cap badges. They also appeared on stationery, timetables and other official publications and were sometimes embodied in the design of office furniture and parcel and newspaper stamps. They could be encountered occasionally in the stonework and ironwork of architectural and civil engineering structures, where some have remained to this day.

In the case of passenger coaches the devices were usually painted on, or made of cast iron or wood and bolted on. In 1856, however, the Birmingham firm of Tearne & Sons Ltd produced the transfer. This offered a cheap, speedy and highly attractive way of displaying a company's insignia in full colour of which advantage was soon taken for the decoration of locomotives as well.

By the turn of the century the use of the armorial transfer had become well established and it was not, incidentally, confined to railways in the British Isles. It was adopted in numerous countries in the world where British capital and enterprise had founded much of the railway systems, and not only in the former Empire. Such countries were Argentina, Bolivia, Brazil, Chile, China, Egypt, Peru, Uruguay and Venezuela, as well as Australia, India, Rhodesia and South Africa.

Sometime before World War II I was given a transfer of the armorial device of the East Indian, a progressive railway to which I had first taken a fancy in my childhood, when it had been represented by one of its handsome 4–4–0 express engines, resplendent in bright terra cotta red livery, in a series of Lambert & Butler cigarette cards entitled *World's Locomotives*. Duly mounted on a plaque of the correct colour, the transfer appealed to me so strongly that I began to collect those of the components of the London & North Eastern, on which my railway career had begun in 1927, and of favourites such as the Midland, the Somerset & Dorset and London & South Western. They made such unusual and striking wall decorations and were so popular with my family that the inevitable happened . . . the collection was extended to include all railways in the British Isles which adopted some form of heraldry as their insignia!

Thirty years ago it was somewhat easier than it is today to form a representative collection of British railway armorial devices. Then there were few collectors and fewer collections. Of the latter, the Pullar Collection in the Station Hotel at Perth, now the backbone of the British Railways Board Collection, and those of the Railway Club, the late A. W. Croughton, Metro-Cammell Ltd and the erstwhile signalling contractors, Tyer & Co Ltd, were probably the five most comprehensive. But all of them, like my own and others of the present day, suffered from the dearth of examples preserved from the years before the advent of the transfer.

Hitherto, anyone interested in the subject has had no work of reference to consult. This book seeks to rectify the situation by offering as complete a picture as it seems possible to create today of a form of ornamentation at which the railways of this country once excelled. It is based upon my own collection, in which most of the transfers have been mounted on plaques painted the appropriate background colour. It is strengthened chiefly from the large private collection of W. H. D. Faulkner, formerly a Director of Tearne & Sons Ltd, and from the British Railways Board Collection, without which a reasonable degree of comprehensiveness could not have been attained. And it has been supplemented by photographs of armorially embellished uniform buttons, most of which once formed part of the late C. F. Dendy Marshall Collection and are now owned by David Swan.

The display of a railway company's initials in script form, particularly on coaches, was a popular practice up to about 1910, but space permits the reproduction of only a handful. Most of those illustrated are very rare examples. Some garters have also been depicted and, to complete the overall picture, a few photographs of parts of armorial devices used really extensively have been included. The wyvern of the Midland, the knot of the North Staffordshire and Britannia of the North Western, to which may be added Eric Gill's totem for the London & North Eastern, became truly universal symbols of the railways they represented.

By comparison, today's symbols, with the honourable exception of the evergreen bar and circle of London Transport, are poor unimaginative substitutes which are unlikely to enjoy longevity.

This book is not in any sense a work on heraldry as such and so heraldic terminology is sparingly employed. When in some appropriate place it is used an explanation is given if the meaning is not obvious. Throughout these pages the descriptions 'left' and 'right' applied to a device are as seen by the beholder and not, as in heraldic parlance, by the bearer.

Only readers who have advanced into their fifties can have witnessed, and may still remember, the last years of the colourful scene before the grouping of railways in the 1920s. One has to be in one's late twenties to have seen anything of the 'Big Four', whose lives ended in long overdue unification in 1948. The number of people interested in railways who have known only the national systems steadily increases.

With this very much in mind each railway dealt with has been given a minute historical sketch and one or two vital statistics added so that the reader can form at least a small mental picture of them. Without this information the book would tend to become a mere catalogue. A few of the smallest railways have not been mentioned at all and this is simply because they are not known to have indulged in any form of heraldic venture save perhaps in their corporate seals.

Audlem
Cheshire
1973

PART ONE

London Midland &
Scottish Railway
and Predecessors

Caledonian Railway

See Supplement p.3

The name *Caledonian Railway* was first used early in 1844, and on 31st July of the following year, after a fierce and protracted Parliamentary struggle costing some £75,000, the company secured its Act of Incorporation. The initial section, from Carlisle to Beattock, was opened to the public on 10th September 1847. And the main line was completed on 15th February 1848, when the sections Beattock–Carstairs–Glasgow and Carstairs–Edinburgh were simultaneously brought into use.

This original Y-shaped system utilised two older lines to reach Glasgow. They were the Wishaw & Coltness (opened in 1841 and acquired eight years later) from Garriongill (12 miles beyond Carstairs) to Coatbridge, and the Glasgow, Garnkirk & Coatbridge (opened in 1831 as the Glasgow & Garnkirk and purchased in 1846) thence to Glasgow.

The Parliamentary session which give birth to the Caledonian also saw the incorporation of the Scottish Central, the Scottish Midland Junction and the Aberdeen Railways, with which communication with Aberdeen was established in 1850. The two last named were merged in 1856 to form the Scottish North Eastern, which in turn was amalgamated with the Caledonian in 1866. The Scottish Central had entered the Caledonian fold the previous year. Various other amalgamations and extensions followed these major mergers of the 1860s and when in 1923 the Caledonian became a constituent company of the LMS it was the second longest railway in Scotland, with a route mileage of 1,114½ and a fleet of 1,070 locomatives, 3,040 coaching vehicles and 51,536 freight vehicles.

Its English ally, the London & North Western, adopted a national emblem, in the shape of Britannia, as a public insignia. The Caledonian went one better and produced a version of the Scottish arms without, so far as is known, getting the blessing of the Lord Lyon, King of Arms. The

13

Scottish railways were just as guilty as those south of the Border in going their own sweet way when it came to armorial bearings!

The Caledonian device appeared as early as July 1865 on the cover of the penny timetables printed for the company by M'Corquodale & Co. This showed a lion *rampant* (i.e. on his hind legs with one of them raised, pawing the air) on a shield beneath which was a riband bearing the motto of the Order of the Thistle *Nemo me impune lacessit—No one provokes me with impunity*. Above the shield was a crest consisting of a helmet surmounted by a crown, and the supporters were the customary unicorns; James IV adopted two unicorns as the supporters of his coat of arms *circa* 1500. This design was changed on the August 1866 timetables to one more akin to the armorial device depicted in the first plate, although the riband did not carry the legend *Caledonian Railway Company*.

Caledonian 2nd device
W. H. D. Faulkner Collection

It is not known when the first armorial transfer (size 15½ in. wide × 9½ in. high), which is reproduced on the purple brown of the lower panels of the coaches, was brought into use. But in September 1888 the Caledonian timetables (still costing a penny) carried a new version of the company's device in which its title appeared on a riband. There were also other differences. A lion *séjant* (sitting), erect and *affronté* (facing the beholder) was now superimposed on the crest, above which was the inscription *In Defence*. From the base of the shield was suspended a medallion of St Andrew. Most extraordinary of all was the spelling of *lacessit* in the motto with an 'e' instead of an 'i'.

This latter curiosity was also to be seen in the second armorial transfer (size 13¼ in. wide × 11 in. high), also illustrated, which it is thought made its first appearance in 1888.

According to the late Comyn Macgregor of the LMS Divisional Engineer's Office in Glasgow, who made a study of Caledonian heraldic matters, the September 1888 design remained on the timetable covers until September 1921. But the second transfer was replaced by a third and final design by Tearnes in September 1899, which is shown on the locomotive Prussian blue. It will be seen that minor changes in colour had been made, notably a white riband tinted pink, replacing one of pink. And *lacessit* was now spelled correctly. The specimen illustrated measures 16⅜ in. wide × 14 in. high; there were two smaller versions 13⅜ in. wide × 11½ in. high and 9½ in. wide × 8½ in. high of exactly the same design.

A short line with a long title, the 6 mile Perth, Almond Valley & Methven, appears to be the only ancestor company of the Caledonian to

Perth, Almond Valley & Methven device
BRB Collection

have left an emblem for posterity. This railway was incorporated in 1856 to build a line from the Scottish Midland Junction, near Dunkeld Road, to Methven in the county of Perth. It owned a solitary locomotive and its rolling stock was supplied by the Scottish North Eastern, by which it was absorbed in 1864.

Its device, made of copper, featured the shield of the City of Perth and embodied the motto *Pro rege, lege et grege—For the king, the law, the people.* The use to which it was put is not known.

Furness Railway

The first section of the Furness Railway, from Barrow and Piel pier to the Dalton mines and Kirkby quarries, was opened on 12th August 1846, two years after its Act of Incorporation. Eventually the company grew into a compact system of 158 route miles, reaching Whitehaven in the north and Carnforth in the east, there to connect with lines owned jointly with the North Western and Midland respectively. It also owned Barrow docks and eight steamers serving Lakes Windermere and Coniston.

Indian red was the distinctive colour adopted for the 136 locomotives. It will be seen from Plate 1 that the backgrounds to the company's title upper panels, worn by the 361 coaching vehicles. And because of the contrast there were appropriate differences in colour between the emblems which embellished locomotives and coaches alike.

It will be seen from Plate I that the backgrounds to the company's title and to the figures in the locomotive design were reddish brown and grey. In the coach design these were changed to blue and sepia. Both measured $9\frac{1}{4}$ in. in diameter.

The Furness device was one of the few displayed by railways to have a religious connotation, being a facsimile of the seal used by Roger Pele, who became Abbot of Furness in 1532. Beneath a canopy the Virgin Mother holds a globe in her right hand to indicate that she is Queen of the World. Her left hand supports the infant Christ. The shields supported by the monks exhibit the lions of England on the right and those of Lancaster on the left. The fearsome looking creature below is said to be a wyvern and the badge of the second Earl of Lancaster. The motto *Cavendo Tutus—Secure by Caution*, is that of the Duke of Devonshire, the seventh Earl and his son being successively Chairman of the company.

One of the gilt uniform buttons, which carried a replica of the device, is illustrated opposite.

Furness gilt uniform button (23mm dia)
David Swan Collection

Glasgow & South Western Railway

Although the Glasgow & South Western contained the oldest railway in
Scotland, the erstwhile 4 ft. gauge horse-operated Kilmarnock & Troon
'plate' railway, it was a little younger than the Caledonian. It was born by
the vesting of the Glasgow, Dumfries & Carlisle (incorporated in 1846)
in the Glasgow, Paisley, Kilmarnock & Ayr (incorporated in 1837 and
opened from Glasgow to Ayr in 1840). The Act of 9th July 1847 which
sanctioned the takeover laid it down that the name *Glasgow & South
Western Railway* should be assumed the day the Glasgow, Dumfries &
Carlisle was opened throughout, when that company would be dissolved.
This event took place on 28th October 1850.

   The newly formed company then adopted the distinctive emblem of the
Glasgow, Paisley, Kilmarnock & Ayr, reproduced in Plate 2. Surrounded
by a garter carrying the name were the caduceus or wand of Mercury, the
messenger of the gods, symbolising speedy transport; a distaff, with the
lint upon it, representative of Minerva, goddess of handicrafts, to depict
the industries served by the line, occupied the centre; and the trident of

Neptune, god of the sea, to denote the company's interest in ports on the Ayrshire coast, was on the right. All three were encircled by a mural crown. The transfer measures 11¾ in. wide × 15¼ in. high.

This device was to be seen in a variety of places, on gilt uniform buttons, hotel chamber pots and official publications to mention only three. A splendid example was embodied in the mosaic paving of the entrance hall floor of the St Enoch Station Hotel in Glasgow. Yet, so far as is known, it never appeared on any of the locomotives, although it is believed that a few coaches once carried it. Here it should be mentioned that the Glasgow & South Western was a 'green' line so far as locomotives were concerned. Coaches were also painted green up to 1884, when the beautiful crimson lake livery of its English ally, the Midland Railway, was adopted.

Early illustrations of the locomotives show the display of the engine numbers within a garter carrying the company's initials, embellishments which were painted on. Tearnes produced two garter transfers, one red and the other pale green, both edged in gold and both carrying the full name in gold. It is thought that these were introduced before 1884, the former being intended for locomotives and the other, which is reproduced, for coaching stock. Garters went out of fashion after the appointment of James Manson as Locomotive Superintendent in 1890.

The second photograph illustrates a hand painted armorial device which was considered in the early days of the company but never introduced, probably because it was too elaborate.

It will be seen that the former emblem of the Glasgow, Paisley, Kilmarnock & Ayr Railway occupies the central position on an ornamental six-sided shield. Glasgow is denoted above it by a shield which depicts an oak tree on a silver field, with a salmon holding a signet ring in its mouth at the base, a robin redbreast at the top and a handbell hanging from the branches, all of which *charges* are associated with legends of the city. The crest consists of a helmet, above which is set the half length figure of St Kentigern (also known as St Mungo) with a crozier in his left hand. Two salmon, each holding a signet ring in its mouth, act as supporters.

On the left of Glasgow a shield carrying a three-masted sailing ship, with a quay in the foreground, represents Greenock. Opposite is the shield of Paisley, on which the figure of St Mirren, holding a crozier in his right hand, stands between three escutcheons. The left hand escutcheon is of gold, with a blue and silver chequered *fess*, the arms of Stewart; the right hand escutcheon, which is surcharged on the trunk of an uprooted oak tree, is a red shield with two silver *cinquefoils* and an escallop shell, the arms of Hamilton; and the escutcheon at the base is an azure shield bearing three covered golden cups, the arms of Shaw.

The supporters of the central hexagonal shield are typical of Scottish

Royal heraldry. On the left, a crowned silver unicorn chained and bearing a shield dependent from its collar; and on the right a crowned, golden brown lion *rampant*, which was to be found on a seal of Alexander II as far back as 1235.

Glasgow & South Western coach garter
W. H. D. Faulkner Collection

Glasgow & South Western unadopted device
BRB Collection

Six more shields, three above and three below a scroll bearing the company's name, make up the rest of the design. The first of the former is beneath a hoof of the unicorn, and consists of a triple-towered silver castle

Glasgow & South Western gilt uniform button
(25mm dia)

Glasgow & South Western chamber pot

on a red background, representing Ayr. Next, centrally above the scroll, is a mitred Archangel Michael, with a crozier in his left hand and a serpent at his feet, to denote Dumfries. Then, under the lion's paw, is the azure shield of Kilmarnock, crossed by a central curved band of red and silver chequers, with a crest formed by a man's right hand open and upright but with the third and fourth fingers folded down.

Underneath the scroll, on the left, is the shield of Girvan, surmounted by a mural crown and bearing a three-masted ship. Centrally, at the base of the achievement, is the old version of the arms of Carlisle, consisting of a golden lion on a red background at the top of the shield; then a golden castle, between two golden roses, on a green background, resting upon alternate wavy bars of silver and blue. Finally, on the right, a shield bearing a three-towered gateway between three crosses represents Sanquhar.

When the Glasgow & South Western ended its independent existence at the end of 1922 it had a route mileage of 493½ and a fleet of 528 locomotives, 1,604 passenger vehicles and 19,252 goods vehicles.

Highland Railway

See supplement p. 4

Farthest north constituent company of the LMS, the Highland originated with the Inverness & Nairn, formally opened on 5th November 1855. Uniting with an extension to Keith to become the Inverness & Aberdeen Junction, a subsequent merger with the Inverness & Perth Junction produced the Highland Railway, which was authorised by an Act of 29th June 1865. Further amalgamations created a system of 506 route miles, mainly single track, which stretched from Keith to Kyle of Lochalsh and from Stanley Junction to Thurso and owned 173 locomotives, 789 coaching vehicles and 2,718 freight vehicles.

In its heraldic device the company embodied the arms of the City of Perth, which it entered from the north over the metals of the Caledonian from Stanley Junction, and those of the Burgh of Inverness, where its headquarters were located. In consequence, it had a strong religious connotation, like the emblem of the Furness, as will be seen from the plate. The shield of the Royal Burgh of Perth carries a Paschal Lamb and that of the town of Inverness our Lord upon the Cross. The transfer measures 9⅞ in. wide × 12¾ in. high and is shown mounted on the shade of green the coaches were painted at the turn of the century.

This design was also to be seen on gilt uniform buttons, one of which is illustrated.

In 1907, when the coaching livery was a plain bronze green, the company decided upon a varnished teak external finish for some sleeping

Highland uniform button (25mm dia)

Highland coach garter
Metro-Cammell Ltd Collection

cars constructed that year by Hurst, Nelson & Co of Motherwell. These vehicles were embellished each end with the plain garter reproduced, which appeared on other coaching stock. Some 3rd class saloons built afterwards were given the same finish, but it was abandoned during World War I, when the sleeping cars and saloons were given the standard livery of bronze green.

The last Deputy Chairman of the Highland was A. E. Pullar of Perth, whose collection of railway heraldic devices is now preserved by the British Railways Board at its Clapham Museum.

Lancashire & Yorkshire Railway

See Supplement p. 4

One of our earliest main lines was the Manchester & Leeds Railway, which was first mooted as long ago as 1825. The company was eventually incorporated in 1836, brought into use by instalments and finally opened throughout on 1st March 1841. It left an armorial imprint for posterity at the south end of the Summit West tunnel, near Littleborough. Carved in the stone above the portal are the arms of Manchester and Leeds, together with the year of the completion of the tunnel, 1839.

To the north a small group of railways, headed by the Manchester, Bury & Rossendale, were consolidated in 1845 to form the East Lancashire Railway. Its headquarters were in Bury, and at Bolton Street station there were to be seen two fine cast iron armorial devices on the entrance gates, resplendent in gold leaf and vermilion. The red rose of Lancaster was the crest and beneath, on an ornamental shield, were three gold lions, similar to those of the Duchy of Lancaster, on a vermilion shield. Nearby, carved in sandstone and mounted on an abutment of Bolton Street bridge, the rose *motif* was repeated within a garter inscribed *Celeritate et utilitate— Speed and usefulness* above a monogram of the company's initials.

When Bolton Street station was modernised in the 1950s the cast iron devices had to be removed. The Author, then Public Relations & Publicity Officer of the London Midland Region, arranged for one to be refixed in the new booking hall and for its companion to be placed in the safekeeping of the British Railways Curator of Historial Relics.

On 9th July 1847 the Manchester & Leeds took over the Wakefield, Pontefract & Goole and the Ashton, Stalybridge & Liverpool Junction Railways and rechristened itself the Lancashire & Yorkshire Railway. The East Lancashire was absorbed twelve years later.

In 1871 the West Lancashire Railway was incorporated to build a line from Southport to Preston, which was finally brought into use throughout in 1882. Tearnes produced an armorial transfer for the company, of which

Manchester & Leeds in stone on tunnel portal
Photo: John Marshall

East Lancashire, cast iron for gates

fortunately a specimen has survived. It measures $9\frac{1}{2}$ in. wide $\times$ $11\frac{7}{8}$ in. high and consists simply of the arms of Lancaster superimposed on an eight-pointed star, the whole encircled by a garter bearing the title of the railway. The date this design was printed is not known, but it cannot have been later than 1897 for in July of that year the West Lancashire, and its satellite the Liverpool, Southport & Preston Junction, were absorbed by the Lancashire & Yorkshire.

Three armorial transfers were produced by Tearnes for the L & Y. Basically they are identical, consisting of two oval shields within a garter bearing the company's name. The lefthand shield displays the arms of Lancaster and the righthand those of York. Above them is a crown and beneath them a red rose and a white rose are entwined.

Lancashire & Yorkshire early device
W. H. D. Faulkner Collection

The earliest design was surrounded by a mass of ornamentation and neither the date of its first appearance nor the use to which it was put are known. It measures 21½ in. wide × 17 in. high. The two other designs were produced at the end of May 1898 and both are devoid of external ornamentation. They differ only in the lettering and colour of the garter. One embodies an Oxford blue garter with gilt *serif* lettering shaded black; it was displayed on the locomotives, all of which were black, chiefly the passenger classes. The other features a pale reddish brown garter with gilt *sans serif* lettering, shaded sepia; this was to be seen on the coaching stock, which was painted dark reddish brown below the waist and light brown above. Both designs measure 10¼ in. wide × 13½ in. high.

On the basis of annual net receipts the L & Y ranked fifth among the British railways with £2·6 million to its credit; and so far as originating 1st class passengers were concerned its tally of 1·9 million a year was eclipsed only by the Caledonian. From its headquarters at Hunts Bank, Manchester, was controlled a closely knit, compact system of 601 route miles on which ran a fleet of 1,650 locomotives, 18 steam rail motors, 4,310 coaching stock units, 119 electric motor cars, 122 trailer cars and 34,670 goods vehicles.

Assigned to the North Western, Midland & West Scottish group, the L & Y was always regarded as a constituent company of the LMS although in fact it was amalgamated with the London & North Western, under the latter's name, a year before grouping. But if there was any doubt as to which took over which, the average Lanky man could be relied upon to give an emphatic and characteristic answer!

Lancashire & Yorkshire gilt uniform button (19mm dia)
David Swan Collection

London & North Western Railway

When the London & North Western was created on 16th July 1846 by the amalgamation of the London & Birmingham, Grand Junction and Manchester & Birmingham Railways it possessed 420 miles of line and was, at the time, the largest system in the United Kingdom. One of its components, the London & Birmingham, which was finally opened throughout between Euston (then Euston Square) station in London and Curzon Street station in Birmingham on 17th September 1838, enjoyed the distinction of being the first trunk line to serve the Metropolis.

As its armorial device the London & Birmingham adopted the arms of the cities in its name. It was to be seen on some of the passenger vehicles, two beautiful specimens being emblazoned on the sides of Queen Adelaide's coach preserved in the British Railways Board Collection. Amongst other places where it was displayed were upon the several pairs of decorative iron gates which survived at Euston until the work of constructing the present station was begun.

One of these cast iron gate plates is illustrated. In its left half the shield contains the ancient arms of London which became the capital of England . in the 11th century. The red cross represents St George, patron saint of England, and the sword St Paul the Apostle, the patron saint of London, who, according to tradition, was beheaded in Rome. The right half displays the shield of Birmingham without its horizontal band of ermine carrying a mural crown. The four quarters represent the family of de Bermingham, who held the manor in the 13th century, during which period Birmingham became a market town; it attained city status in 1889 when it assumed its coat of arms. Above the shield is a dragon's *sinister* wing, charged with a red cross, the crest of the City of London. The plate measures $8\frac{5}{8}$ in. wide $\times$ $11\frac{7}{8}$ in. high.

The Grand Junction was incorporated in 1833 and absorbed the Warrington & Newton at the same time. When it was opened in 1837 it extended from Newton, on the Liverpool & Manchester, to Birmingham, on the London & Birmingham, serving Warrington, Stafford and Wolver- hampton *en route*. It purchased the Chester & Crewe in 1840, the year the latter was opened, and absorbed the Liverpool & Manchester in 1845. These acquisitions are reflected in the hand-painted device adopted in the last twelve months of its separate existence; the shield is quartered by Liverpool, Manchester, Chester and Birmingham.

Third component of the North Western, the Manchester & Birmingham, ran from Manchester to the Grand Junction at Crewe, and was opened in 1842. Although it never reached Birmingham its armorial device inevitably consisted of the two cities named in its title and a good hand-painted specimen may be seen in the British Railways Board Collection. The example illustrated is in the form of a metal plaque which was made for display at the Manchester terminus. For many years it occupied a commanding position in the North Western, later LMS, booking hall at London Road station (which was shared with the Great Central, later LNER) and today it is embodied in the external fabric of the modernised station, now known as Piccadilly.

Four railways which entered the LNWR fold deserve mention because in each case they left behind them armorial reminders of their existence.

London & Birmingham in cast iron

First to be acquired was the Huddersfield & Manchester Railway & Canal Company, taken over in 1847, whose device consisting of the arms of Huddersfield and Manchester was carved in sandstone over the former LNWR booking office at Huddersfield station and is still to be seen there.

Grand Junction painted device
BRB Collection

Manchester & Birmingham in metal

Huddersfield & Manchester in stone
Photo: John Marshall

Chester & Holyhead stone monogram
Photo: T. Noble

The lefthand shield portrays Huddersfield activities by a fleece representing woollen textiles and a beehive allusive to industry in general. It bears no resemblance to the present arms of the county borough of Huddersfield and may well be the only remaining example extant.

Next to follow, in 1858, was the Chester & Holyhead, half of whose capital had been subscribed by the London & Birmingham and Grand Junction Railways and whose monogram has survived in the stonework of Bangor station.

Two years later the South Staffordshire, which possessed a main line from Wichnor junction, on the Midland, to Dudley, via Lichfield and Walsall, was leased to the LNWR. An example of its extravagant hand-painted armorial device has, fortunately, been preserved in the Metro-Cammell Ltd Collection. The most unusual feature of the design, which was to be seen on the first class carriages, is the central shield which, with the crown above, represents Walsall; it is taken from the 15th century seal of the Corporation, which bore the then Royal arms of England (three lions) and France (three *fleurs-de-lis*) quarterly. The left and right hand shields portray Dudley castle and Lichfield cathedral respectively.

Cromford & High Peak on tunnel portal

The last was the Cromford & High Peak, a remarkable line incorporated in 1825 to connect the Cromford Canal with the Peak Forest Canal at Whaley Bridge, reaching a summit level of 1,266 feet at Ladmanlow. This was achieved by a number of rope worked inclined planes, with intervening sections operated by horses. It was opened in 1830 and the north

31

portal of Newhaven tunnel under the Ashbourne–Buxton road, near Parsley Hay, was inscribed with the emblem illustrated, which was almost a replica of the company's seal. Locomotives eventually displaced horses on the line, which was absorbed by the LNWR in 1887.

Britannia was adopted by the LNWR as its emblem, a compliment to its ancestor, the Liverpool & Manchester, on whose share certificates the lady was conspicuous in a pose both statuesque and smacking of an over-dressed policewoman on point duty. In the various LNWR versions, however, she was usually seated, protected by her Union Jack shield and companion lion; in some cases, as on nickel uniform buttons and stationery, there was also a train on a viaduct in the background.

The early hand-painted Britannia emblems, one of which is preserved in the British Railways Board Collection, served as the pattern for the transfers ultimately produced by Tearnes, of which three different types are known. The first reproduced was displayed on the coaching stock, which was finished in purple lake with spilt milk upper panels; it measures 9½ in. wide × 9½ in. high. The second embellished many of the black locomotives, mainly passenger classes, but it was also to be seen on the middle splashers of a numerous batch of 0-6-0 goods engines built between 1880 and 1902 which in consequence were nicknamed *Cauliflowers*. This transfer measures 13⅜ in. across the widest part of its typical Victorian ornamentation and is 12½ in. high. A smaller variant of exactly the same colouring, 8⅜ in. wide × 6¼ in. high, was displayed on some of the road vehicles. The third design, a very simple affair, was produced for steamships, and has a diameter of only 16½ in. The background of the garter is dark navy blue, the four 'jewels' in the garter and the background of Britannia and her lion are red, and the whole of the remainder is gilt.

In Ireland the LNWR owned the 5 ft. 3 in. gauge Dundalk, Newry & Greenore Railway, which was publicly opened between Dundalk and Greenore on 1st May 1873; the Newry–Greenore section was brought into use on 1st August 1876, raising the total route mileage of this Irish outpost to 26¾.

The LNWR provided the whole of the locomotives and rolling stock, which followed the traditions of Crewe and Wolverton both as regards design and colours, but the little system was given its own armorial device, which adorned the carriages. It will be seen that Britannia (standing, for a change) clasps hands with Hibernia, complete with harp and accompanied by an Irish greyhound, to symbolise the advent of an English railway on Irish soil. Britannia, incidentally, has shed her shield and lost her lion! In the background there is a train on the left, a paddle steamer between the two national figures, and the pier and lighthouse at Greenore on the right.

Two designs were produced by Tearnes, both measuring 15⅛ in.

See supplement p. 4

Caledonian 1st device
W. H. D. Faulkner Collection

Caledonian final device

Furness (locomotives)

Furness (coaches)
W. H. D. Faulkner Collection

PLATE 1

Highland

West Lancashire
W. H. D. Faulkner Collection

Glasgow & South Western
BRB Collection

Lancashire & Yorkshire (coaches)
W. H. D. Faulkner Collection

Lancashire & Yorkshire (locomotives)

PLATE 2

London & North Western steamship device

London & North Western nickel uniform button
(25mm dia)
David Swan Collection

wide × 12¾ in. high, but it is not known when one replaced the other. At a glance they appear to be identical, but there are subtle differences, the most noticeable being the replacement of the shaggy grey Irish greyhound in the earlier design by a somewhat sleeker, blue-black specimen in the later (in North Western loco livery, obviously!). The train, too, is changed; in the first design it consists of a smoking 2-2-2 with 6-wheeled tender and 4-wheeled coach; in the second a smokeless 4-4-0 with 4-wheeled tender and bogie coach are to be seen.

In 1933 the working of the line was taken over by the Great Northern of Ireland and on the last day of 1951, after most protracted legal and other processes, it was closed down.

The biggest amalgamation in the life of the London & North Western before grouping was the merger with the Lancashire & Yorkshire, which became effective as from 1st January 1922. Before this took place it possessed a route mileage of over 2,066, a fleet of 3,336 locomotives, 9,551 coaching vehicles, 7 steam and 1 petrol rail motors, 73 electric motor coaches, 112 trailer coaches and 75,674 freight vehicles. By clever use of the advertising tag *The Premier Line*, it convinced some people that it *was* the premier line, which it certainly was not, although it was a great railway in many ways.

Midland Railway

The amalgamation of the North Midland, Midland Counties and Birmingham & Derby Junction Railways to form the Midland, the Act for which received the Royal Assent on 10th May 1844, was the first merger of note in railway history. It set an example which was soon to be followed elsewhere.

Derby station was the meeting place of the three railways. In the supports of its roof were embodied curved cast iron armorial plaques 20 in. wide × 19 in. high, of which a specimen is illustrated. Several of these remained *in situ* until the reconstruction of the station in the early 1950s and extensive enquiries made at the time of their removal pointed to the likelihood that they afford an example of allusive heraldry. The chevron probably represents the roof of the station, the roundel beneath it the owner, the North Midland, and the two roundels above it the tenants, the Midland Counties and the Birmingham & Derby Junction.

The North Midland was another of our early trunk railways, being incorporated in 1836 for the construction of a main line from Derby to Leeds. It was opened in two instalments four years later, the second being brought into use on 30th June 1840.

See Hamilton Ellis "The Trains we Loved" p 33 for a query and remark about the MR c/la. He also remarks on others

Derby station cast iron device

North Midland in cast iron for coaches

Midland Counties painted device
BRB Collection

Birmingham & Derby Junction in metal

An example of the neat metal armorial device displayed on the company's first class carriages is reproduced. It measures 6¼ in. wide × 7½ in. high, its *bas-relief* design giving it a maximum depth of 1¼ in. Both the crest, which is an owl, and the upper half of the shield, which displays three mullets and a fleece, are taken from the arms of Leeds. The lower half is shared by Derby and Derbyshire. The stag within the palings on the left, often referred to locally as 'the buck in the park', has been used to represent Derby for hundreds of years and, it is understood, was granted by Richard II in 1378, being confirmed by Letters Patent in 1637. The Tudor rose on the right has always been associated with the county of Derby, often in conjunction with a Royal or Imperial crown; the initials AR stand for Adelaide Regina, consort of William IV during whose reign the North Midland was created.

In the hand-painted replica of the Midland Counties arms the same device denoting Derbyshire has been embodied, but with three roses instead of one. The other components are Leicester (top left), Nottingham (top right) and Warwick (bottom right). The pierced *cinquefoil* of Leicester was the emblem of Robert Fitzpernell, Earl of Leicester, who died in 1204; the Nottingham device is taken from the town arms in use before the creation of Nottingham as a city in 1897; and Warwick is represented by its 14th century seal, which is taken from the arms of the Beauchamp Earls of Warwick.

The Midland Counties Railway was incorporated in 1836, its final main line section from Leicester to Rugby being brought into use on 1st July 1840. When the first section from Nottingham to Derby was formally opened on 30th May 1839 the cards of invitation to the ceremony and the panels of the carriages bore the company's coat of arms. And when the second section from Trent junction, on the Nottingham–Derby line, to Leicester was opened on 4th May 1840 the cast iron bridge over the river Trent was decorated with the quarters of the device in the form of four separate cast iron shields, one each above the two river piers. The bridge was replaced by the present steel girder structure early in this century, when the four shields were recovered and embodied in the stonework parapet of the new bridge, one each end either side of the track, where they have remained to this day.

Also incorporated in 1836, the Birmingham & Derby Junction was publicly opened on 12th August 1839 between Derby and Hampton, whence its trains ran into Birmingham over the metals of the London & Birmingham. This was soon found to be a highly unsatisfactory arrangement, and its own line from Whitacre into Birmingham, authorised in 1840, was brought into use on 10th February 1842.

Like the North Midland, the B & DJ displayed a cast metal device on its carriages, the body colours of which were: first class, bright yellow; second class, blue; third class, dark brown. It will be seen from the illustration that the design consists of the arms of the two places in the company's title. The panel is 14¾ in. square and as its *bas-relief* treatment gives it a depth of some 1½ in. it is altogether a rather massive emblem. An example of this coat of arms in stone could once be seen in the upper part of the west side of Derby station buildings at the south end.

The first armorial transfers of the Midland appear to have been produced by Tearnes in the early 1880s, the design closely resembling a diamond-shaped hand-painted device preserved in the British Railways Board Collection. There were two versions, one in which the ornamentation immediately adjacent to the outer edge of the scroll bearing the title was tinted green with gold highlights, and the other in which the same ornamentation was light blue shaded dark blue. The first was displayed on locomotives, which were then given an apple green livery (the famous crimson lake was not adopted until the end of 1883); the other ornamented the coaching stock, which had worn crimson lake since the close of the 1860s.

There were some unusual features about the components of the shield, which had a dolphin and a salamander as supporters and which portrayed six of the principal towns originally served by the Midland—Birmingham, Derby, Bristol (left to right, top row) and Leicester, Lincoln, Leeds (left to right, beneath). Birmingham lacked its horizontal bar of ermine and its second and third quarters were unaccountably reversed; the stag of Derby looked *backwards* within a *walled* park; and the ship of Bristol looked rather odd riding upon natural as well as heraldic water!

These discrepancies were repeated in the second design which was produced in the same two versions when the first was abandoned in 1891. This second design differed only in the arrangement of the title on the scroll, which was altered to read *RAILWAY MIDLAND COMPANY* so as to bring *MIDLAND* above the shield.

Although a small size, 5 in. wide × 4 in. high, is known to have existed, these early diamond-shaped armorial transfers usually measured 14 in. wide × 13½ in. high. Frequently, two would adorn each side of the opulent looking carriages, whether 4-wheeled, 6-wheeled or bogie vehicles. But so far as the locomotives were concerned their use from 1887 onwards was confined to the leading splashers of all single-framed 2-4-0 and 4-4-0 passenger tender engines and to the splashers of the then new 4-2-2 express locomotives until 1905.

One would have expected to see a legless wyvern, the true emblem of the Midland, embodied in the design as it was in the company's ambulance medals and elsewhere. This somewhat fearsome looking heraldic beast was the crest of Thomas of Lancaster, second Lancastrian Earl of Leicester and, earlier still, was said to be the badge of the ancient kingdom of Mercia, of which Leicester was the principal town. Inevitably it became the crest of the Leicester coat of arms, wherein it is shown with outstretched wings. The Leicester & Swannington Railway adopted the wyvern as a crest, although for what purpose is not known (it did not appear on the seal) and after the Midland had purchased the line in 1846 it was increasingly used as the insignia of that company. And very appropriately too, for the Leicester & Swannington, incorporated as long ago as 29th May 1830 and first opened on 17th July 1832, was the oldest railway component of the Midland.

Midland 1st device for locomotives
W. H. D. Faulkner Collection

A few of the numerous places into which the wyvern was introduced are illustrated. In the case of passenger coaches, although it was often to be seen in compartment luggage rack supports and sometimes in the opaque glass windows of lavatory compartments, its display in transfer form seems to have been limited to the exterior of a few dining carriages, of which No 359, built in 1892, was an example. One of the most unusual places was in the supports of bracket signals at Leicester and Nottingham. When improvements were carried out at these important stations around the turn of the century, intermediate signals were installed on some of the platforms. The directors insisted that they should be decorative and distinctive cast iron brackets embodying the wyvern were the outcome. A pair of them, adapted by the author as a house name sign far from their original habitat, are illustrated on page 12.

Perhaps the most unusual place of all is the tombstone of Cecil W. Paget, son of the onetime Midland Chairman, Sir Ernest Paget, who became General Superintendent of the company in 1907 and whose greatest achievement was to implement successfully the pioneer installation of traffic control in this country. He was buried in Sutton Bonnington cemetery in December 1936, within a stone's throw of the trains he knew so well.

The wyvern eventually came into its own as the Midland crest when the final armorial transfer, putting right the mistakes and omissions in the previous designs, was adopted in 1906. This transfer is so elegant and so beautifully proportioned that it is surprising that the blessing of the College of Arms was not sought for it. Most unexpectedly, it did not appear on coaching stock (save on a special saloon coach taken over from the London, Tilbury & Southend Railway), which henceforth became devoid of heraldic embellishment as the former armorial transfers were painted out. But it was to be seen on passenger and goods tender engines alike, either on the rear splashers or cab sides, and on two classes of tank engine, the 0-6-4Ts of 1907 and the 4-6-4Ts built for the London, Tilbury & Southend in 1912. It was also worn by the crimson lake and white electric tramcars of the Burton & Ashby Light Railway. And, *mirabile dictu*, it was retained on goods tender engines when unlined black was adopted as their livery in 1910.

On 1st July 1903 the Midland added to its hopes and responsibilities by acquiring the Belfast & Northern Counties, a prosperous Irish railway which had been incorporated in 1845 as the Belfast & Ballymena. Its first section was opened in 1848 and the title *Belfast & Northern Counties Railway* was assumed twelve years later. By a succession of amalgamations it developed into a compact system of $265\frac{1}{4}$ route miles, of which $63\frac{1}{2}$ were on the 3 ft. gauge; the remainder was, of course, built to the standard Irish gauge of 5 ft. 3 in.

For one of the companies absorbed, the Ballymena & Larne, taken over in 1889, Tearnes produced a transfer of its monogram within a garter, 18 in. wide × 15 in. high, bearing the legend *Ballymena and Larne Ry. Co.* No specimen appears to have survived.

The Belfast & Northern Counties itself adopted the achievement of Belfast *in toto* as its heraldic device, the earliest known example of which is preserved in the Metro-Cammell Ltd Collection. This is probably a replica of the design once displayed on the carriages, some of which were also decorated with the company's monogram at each end. Tearnes recorded a transfer printed in December 1898 and, in fact, two quite

Midland gilt cap badge for senior uniformed staff

Midland luggage rack support

Wyverns in Avon bridge at Weston, Bath

Obverse of Midland silver ambulance medal

Midland nickel uniform button (17mm dia)

Chamber pot wyvern

Belfast & Northern Counties painted device for coaches
Metro-Cammell Ltd Collection

Belfast & Northern Counties device for locomotives

different designs have been traced. The most elaborate, embodying voluminous mantling beneath the crest, was for application to the locomotives, which were painted a deep laurel green. But, so far as is known, only a handful of the 4-4-0 express engines carried it on their leading splashers. The other design, which measures $14\frac{1}{8}$ in. wide $\times$ $12\frac{1}{4}$ in. high, was worn by the mail vans.

NCC monogram used by Midland

After the Midland take-over the system became known as the Northern Counties Committee, with a management committee sitting at Belfast. A monogram transfer $15\frac{1}{2}$ in. wide $\times$ 11 in. high was introduced at this time, chiefly for coaching stock (including steam rail motors) to supplement the Midland diamond-shaped armorial transfer.

There was a curious revival of the last-named. It was applied to the leading splashers of two NCC 4-4-0 express locomotives built at Derby in 1914 and two further 4-4-0 and 0-6-0 locomotives completed a few years later.

By an Act of 7th August 1912 the Midland absorbed the London, Tilbury & Southend, which had been incorporated sixty years earlier. It was a well run little system, with a fleet of 82 locomotives, all but two of them tank engines, wearing a light green livery, and 561 coaching vehicles with varnished teak bodies.

Two early transfers of a simple armorial device, one for the locomotives and the other for the coaches, were produced before 1890 and differed only in minor details. The central feature was the gateway of Tilbury fort, originally a blockhouse built by Henry VIII for the defence of the Thames

London, Tilbury & Southend 1st device for locomotives
BRB Collection

London, Tilbury & Southend 1st device for coaches
BRB Collection

and the venue for Elizabeth's review of her troops in 1588 at the time of the Armada.

The third and final transfer, which has a diameter of 11½ in. and was designed in the company's works at Plaistow, retained Tilbury fort gateway and flanked it with shields denoting London and Essex; at the base a third shield bearing a white horse on a red ground represented Kent. The latter was justified by the fact that the LT & S operated the ferry service between Tilbury and Gravesend from its own piers and with its own vessels. Six paddle steamers were in operation and these were also used as tenders for taking passengers to and from liners in the river off Tilbury.

When the Midland became a constituent company of the LMS it had grown to be the third longest railway in the British Isles, and in most ways was the best of them all. It served more towns and cities than any other and shared only with the LNWR the distinction of owning lines in England, Scotland, Wales and Ireland. Over its 2,169½ route miles ran a fleet of 3,019 steam locomotives, 6,019 coaching vehicles and 107,617 freight vehicles, supplemented by an electric battery locomotive, 48 electric motor cars, 49 trailer cars and 20 electric trams. It enjoyed an enviable record of pioneering achievement and, because of their general efficiency and excellence, Midland locomotive and carriage designs and hotel, catering and publicity methods were to dominate LMS practice for many years after grouping.

North Staffordshire Railway

Amongst the smaller railways the North Staffordshire was probably one of the most individualistic and it was certainly the equal of its bigger contemporaries in the architectural design of its stations. Arnold Bennett was inspired to include it in his writings of the Potteries and in recent years it has earned the unique distinction of having a successful musical documentary produced about its life and times, bearing a title that was its own nickname—*The Knotty*.

The North Staffordshire began in 1846, when it was authorised to build a main line from Macclesfield to Colwich via Stoke-on-Trent, with branches from Harecastle to Crewe, from Stoke-on-Trent to Newcastle and from Stone to Norton Bridge. Other lines to Sandbach, to Leek and to Uttoxeter were planned and the first section, from Stoke-on-Trent to Stone and Norton Bridge, was formally opened on 17th April 1848. By new construction and amalgamation it grew steadily into a tight little network of 220½ route miles and when it became a constituent of the LMS it brought with it a well maintained stud of 192 locomotives, together with an electric battery locomotive, 3 steam rail motors, 534 coaching vehicles and 6,248 freight vehicles.

From the beginning it used as its emblem the Staffordshire knot, from which its nickname was derived, and adopted the arms of the town of Stafford as its armorial device. The earliest example of the latter is doubtless the stone achievement in the balcony in the front of the central gable of the station building at Stoke-on-Trent. It is still in a good state of preservation, as will be seen from the photograph.

North Staffordshire in stone

Up to the middle 1870s, when the first transfer of the armorial device was produced, the knot was painted on locomotives and carriages alike. Elsewhere it appeared on wagons and canal barges (the North Staffordshire was the third largest canal owning company), staff uniforms and official publications, clocks and furniture. The knot was also produced in transfer form for the locomotives and carriages, and a monogram transfer of the letters NSR was manufactured for the latter, but specimens of neither appear to have survived.

The neat armorial transfer with which all the madder lake locomotives and coaching vehicles were adorned at the time the line became part of the LMS is reproduced. It measures 11 in. wide × 16 in. high and the

South Staffordshire painted device
Metro-Cammell Ltd Collection

London & North Western (coaches)

London & North Western (locomotives)

Dundalk, Newry & Greenore 1st device
BRB Collection

PLATE 3

Midland 2nd device (coaches)

Midland final device

Belfast & Northern Counties (mail vans)

London, Tilbury & Southend final device

PLATE 4

only difference between it and the first design is the colour of the background to the company's title; in the original transfer it was dark emerald green.

There was a smaller version of the blue gartered transfer $7\frac{3}{8}$ in. wide $\times$ $10\frac{1}{2}$ in. high, heavily shaded middle green and light green, but it is not known for what purpose it was employed.

North Staffordshire early device
W. H. D. Faulkner Collection

North Staffordshire nickel uniform button (22mm dia)
David Swan Collection

Maryport & Carlisle Railway

There were 27 subsidiary companies in the group of railways which made up the LMS, but only a handful of them owned locomotives and rolling stock.

The oldest was the Maryport & Carlisle, which was incorporated as long ago as 1837. It was opened in instalments and completed throughout on 10th February 1845, eventually owning nearly 43 route miles of line. It enjoyed an enviable dividend record, which rose to a peak of 13 per cent in 1873, and it was one of the most prosperous of all British railways over a long period of years. It contributed 33 locomotives, 71 coaching vehicles and 1,404 freight vehicles to the LMS.

Two early types of transfer for the decoration of the coaching stock, which was given a varnished teak external finish at the time, have been traced. One was a conventional script monogram. The other consisted of the initials *MCR* on a red field surrounded by an Oxford blue garter with the usual gilt edging, ornamentation and legend bearing the full title. It measures 9¼ in. wide × 11¼ in. high over black shading.

Maryport & Carlisle monogram

Maryport & Carlisle garter monogram
W. H. D. Faulkner Collection

A livery of green with white upper panels was adopted in 1905 for the passenger train vehicles, which blended pleasantly with the green of the locomotives. Five years later Tearnes produced for display on both an armorial device which shared with that of the Central London the distinction of embodying neither name nor motto.

The transfer measures 10¼ in. wide × 16¾ in. high and is simple and appropriate. On an ornamental shield Maryport (top left) and Carlisle (bottom right) are quartered with the arms of J. P. Senhouse of Netherall (top right), represented by the popinjay, and those of Sir Wilfrid Lawson (bottom left). Senhouse and Lawson were the first and fourth of the five chairmen the company had during its eighty-five years of life.

Uniform buttons carried the same device.

Maryport & Carlisle nickel uniform button (22mm dia)
David Swan Collection

North London Railway

On 26th August 1846 the ponderously titled East & West India Docks & Birmingham Junction Railway received its Act of Incorporation. This sanctioned the construction of a railway from the London & Birmingham (which had just become a component of the newly formed London & North Western) at Chalk Farm to the West India Docks at Blackwall, 8 miles in length. The name of the company was changed for the better *North London Railway* as from New Year's Day 1853.

These antecedents are reflected in the transfer of the North London armorial device, $8\frac{1}{2}$ in. wide × $10\frac{3}{4}$ in. high, with which the teak finished passenger coaches were embellished. In the top left quarter the anchor, with the shield on its shank emblazoned with a lion *rampant*, denotes the maritime connexion of the railway and was probably adopted by the East

India Dock Company (incorporated in 1803) to symbolise security and strength. Then follow Birmingham, top right, and London, bottom left. The entrance gateway to the West India Import Dock (opened in 1802) occupies the fourth quarter. The East and West India Docks undertakings were amalgamated in 1838, the gateway being taken down in 1932.

Although at the end of 1908 the North London entered into an agreement under which its busy little system of 14¼ route miles was worked by the North Western, it managed to retain a rather precarious independence and duly became a subsidiary company of the LMS, to which it contributed 99 locomotives, 373 passenger vehicles and 297 freight vehicles.

East & West Junction garter

Stratford-on-Avon & Midland Junction Railway

The fusion of three impoverished little railways in the heart of England in 1908 created the Stratford-on-Avon & Midland Junction, which began to function as such on 1st January 1909. Extending from Ravenstone Wood Junction, on the Bedford–Northampton line of the Midland in the east, to Broom Junction, on the Evesham–Redditch line of the same company in the west, the SMJ, with its two branches, owned a route mileage of 67½. There were 13 locomotives, 28 passenger vehicles and 130 freight vehicles.

No armorial device of any kind was in use but the oldest and biggest component, the East & West Junction, which ran from Stratford-on-Avon to Towcester, displayed a garter 12¾ in. wide × 12¼ in. high on some of its chocolate and cream coaches. It is illustrated because of its great rarity; the vehicle number was usually exhibited within it.

According to Tearnes' records this garter transfer was first ordered in 1897, when the white background was shaded pink. Similar transfers ordered nine years later embodied a green background shaded pink. The specimen in the author's collection has a pale blue background.

Wirral gilt uniform button (22mm dia)
David Swan Collection

Cockermouth, Keswick & Penrith
gilt uniform button (17mm dia)
David Swan Collection

Wirral Railway

The Wirral Railway linked Birkenhead Park, Seacombe, New Brighton and West Kirby, each with the others, by nearly 14 route miles of line. All were terminals save Birkenhead Park, where an end-on junction was effected with the Mersey Railway Passenger traffic predominated, there being a stock of 71 coaches to handle it. Locomotives, all tanks, totalled 17, and there were only 80 freight vehicles.

Although it was incorporated as late as 1883, the Wirral embodied a predecessor, the Hoylake Railway, which dated back twenty years earlier.

Some of the stations exhibited the company's emblem, the Wirral bugle horn, in sandstone. This bugle horn is part of the arms of the Borough of Wallasey and was introduced into the heraldic design for Wirral in the reign of Edward III. In the $9\frac{7}{8}$ in. wide × $11\frac{1}{8}$ in. high transfer device displayed on the chocolate coloured coaches and, rather unusually, high up on the cab sides of the black locomotives, a stag's head may be seen. It is believed that this was taken from the arms of the Stanleys of Cheshire. The transfer was first printed in 1891.

Electrification of the Wirral system, save the Seacombe line, was completed by the LMS in 1938 and today it is worked with the former Mersey Railway as one unit.

The only other LMS subsidiary companies to possess locomotives and rolling stock were the Knott End & Garstang and the Cleator & Workington Junction Railways, but neither used any device. Another subsidiary, the Cockermouth, Keswick & Penrith, is worthy of mention. This railway was incorporated in 1861 and opened on 2nd January 1865. The London & North Western and the North Eastern (as successor to the Stockton & Darlington) were each permitted to subscribe £25,000 towards the undertaking and they worked the line between them. But the gilt buttons on station staff uniforms were distinctive in that they bore the embossed monogram *CKPR* and, because of their great rarity, one of them is illustrated.

London Midland & Scottish Railway

After toying with the title *London Midland & Northern*, the North Western, Midland and West Scottish group finally decided upon *London Midland & Scottish*. This was just as big a mouthful and it is not surprising that the euphonious abbreviation *LMS* made its appearance upon locomotives and rolling stock, timetable covers and press advertisements, posters and posterboard headings at an early date. The incomparable Midland crimson lake livery was assumed by passenger locomotives and coaching stock.

What *is* surprising is that the LMS, which had inherited from its two largest constituents, the Midland and the North Western, the distinction of owning lines in the four countries of the United Kingdom, adopted such an uninspiring armorial device. Within a circle of $14\frac{1}{8}$ in. diameter overall were exhibited merely the dragon's wing of London and a rose and thistle *motif* to denote England and Scotland. Butchers and Tearnes were the suppliers.

Smaller versions of this transfer, of 6 in. and $3\frac{1}{2}$ in. diameter, were manufactured by Tearnes for LMS steamships, and in 1931 yet another transfer was produced for the same purpose. This, it will be seen, was oval in shape and measured $3\frac{5}{16}$ in. wide $\times$ $5\frac{7}{8}$ in. high. There was no change in the colours.

Parliamentary powers to provide road transport services were granted the railways in 1928 and the LMS entered into joint bus operation agreements with the four municipalities of Huddersfield, Todmorden, Halifax and Sheffield. The two last-named were, in fact, tripartite agreements, with the LNER making up the trinity. In consequence, numbers of buses in the Huddersfield and Todmorden areas appeared with the emblems of the LMS and the appropriate municipality on their sides, and others in the Halifax area likewise bore the arms of the three partners. These armorial excursions were not emulated at Sheffield, where lettering indicated triple ownership.

London, Midland & Scottish device for steamships
Gerald Hartley Collection

The Huddersfield county borough arms, it will be noted, is quite different from that illustrated in the Huddersfield & Manchester Railway device on page 30. The whole design, consisting of three castles on a chevron, with two rams above and one beneath, is based on the heraldry of the Ramsden family, who have held the Manor of Huddersfield since the reign of Elizabeth I. The transfer measured $14\frac{1}{4}$ in. in diameter. The Todmorden arms were granted when the borough was in both Lancashire and Yorkshire; hence the *fess* denotes the river Calder, the boundary between the two counties, which are represented by a red rose *in chief* and a white rose in the base respectively. The remaining emblems indicate the textile industry. St John the Baptist, patron saint of wool merchants, is the 'holy face' in the centre of the Halifax county borough arms. The Manor was once held by Edward the Confessor; the chequers are from the arms of the Earls of Warenne, who held it in Norman times. The oval transfer is 15 in. wide × 11 in. high.

At the end of 1927 a new arrangement of lettering and numbering was adopted for the locomotives. The number, which was carried on

Todmorden & LMS Joint buses device
Photo: John Marshall

Huddersfield & LMS Joint buses device

tender and tank sides, *à la* Midland, was to be replaced by *LMS* and the emblem (where it was applied) or *LMS* on cab and bunker sides was to give way to the number. Henceforth, with very few exceptions, locomotives ceased to be adorned with any armorial device. Pleasing *sans serif* letters and numerals were introduced on the locomotives in 1936, but in less than two years reversion to the former *serif* characters took place.

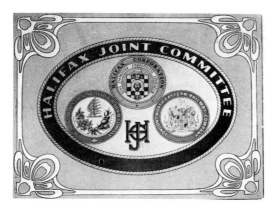

Halifax Joint Committee buses device

See Supplement p.5

During the mid-1930s chrome yellow lining and lettering began to supplant the gilt on some main line coaching stock, as an economy measure, and in 1936 a chrome yellow lined and lettered transfer of the emblem, produced only by Butchers, was brought into use to match the new style. The diameter remained at 14⅛ in. and there were no other colour changes. On dining and sleeping cars gilt lettering and lining-out were retained until 1942 and on these units the original gilt version of the emblem was still used.

In 1946 the LMS began to abandon the crimson lake livery. Black became standard for all locomotives and only the Pacifics and three classes of 4-6-0 express passenger engine were given any lining-out, which was maroon and straw. In the case of the coaching stock, maroon bodies with straw lining, lettering and numbering became the order of the day. A straw lined and lettered version of the emblem was also produced in transfer form, there being no other alteration in colour. The overall diameter of 14⅛ in. was retained.

In twice altering the lining and lettering colours of its armorial transfer to match changes in livery the LMS was almost alone amongst British railway companies.

See Supplement p.5

The letters LMS lend themselves to end-on fusion so as to form a distinctive emblem akin to that so effectively displayed by the Canadian National Railways at the present time. In a carriage diagram map for the London, Tilbury & Southend lines and a poster map of the London suburban lines, both designed by the author and produced by the LMS in 1935, he embodied such an emblem. But the idea was never developed and, apart from some half-hearted attempts by the company's Hotels Department, no other efforts to devise a universal symbol appear to have been made.

London, Midland & Scottish gilt uniform button
(26mm dia)
David Swan Collection

PART TWO

London & North Eastern Railway
and Predecessors

Great Central Railway

See supplement
p. 16

The origin of the Great Central dates back to the Sheffield, Ashton-under-Lyne & Manchester Railway which, with the completion of Britain's then longest tunnel at Woodhead, was finally opened throughout on 23rd December 1845.

From the outset the company's armorial device was painted on the centre door on each side of the 1st and 2nd class coaches, which wore a livery of light claret; the glazed hats of the guards were similarly emblazoned. The device simply consisted of a garter carrying the title and enclosing three shields which, left to right, denoted Sheffield, Ashton-under-Lyne and Manchester.

In 1846 the SA & M was merged with railways under construction or authorised, running eastwards from Sheffield, and with the Grimsby dock undertaking, and from 1st January 1847 began to function as the Manchester, Sheffield & Lincolnshire Railway. The first known transfer of the new company's armorial device was oval in shape and embellished the doors of main line coaches, which were given a teak finish. The transfer measures $6\frac{1}{8}$ in. wide $\times$ 8 in. high and, it will be seen, embodies shields containing parts of the arms of Manchester (ship), Sheffield (arrows), Lincoln (cross and fleur-de-lis), East Retford (two eagles) and Great Grimsby (chevron and three boars' heads). It was still being printed as late as 1888.

By this time a circular design, of which there were two versions, had been brought into use. The same arms were repeated, but rearranged around a rose, thistle and shamrock *motif*. The only difference between the two was in the colour of the garter. The first version contained a white garter which carried gold *serif* letters shaded in light blue; the second had an Oxford blue garter with gold *serif* letters shaded black. Each transfer

63

measures 17¾ in. wide × 15⅞ in. high and both were chiefly to be seen on passenger coaches.

The final MS & L armorial transfer appeared in the early 1890s and was intended for display on the express passenger locomotives. It was circular in shape, measuring 16½ in. wide × 16½ in. high, and basically of the same design as its predecessors, but there were several detail differences. The ornamentation within and without the garter was of a more open pattern, whilst the background inside the garter was maroon instead of red. The gilt lettering on the mainly white garter was outlined in brown and shaded pale blue.

In anticipation of the opening of its extension to Marylebone station in London the MS & L changed its name to *Great Central* as from 1st August 1897. And on 25th February 1898 it made history by being granted a coat of arms by the Garter, Clarenceux and Norroy Kings of Arms, the first railway to achieve this distinction.

Manchester, Sheffield & Lincolnshire 2nd device for
coaches
W. H. D. Faulkner Collection

Great Central coat of arms with Robinson locomotive crest

Wrexham, Mold & Connahs Quay garter

The Great Central must have been fully alive to the fact, for no other railway was so generous in the display of a coat of arms. Soon it was to be seen everywhere on crockery, cutlery and glassware in the company's hotels, refreshment rooms and restaurant cars. Tankards and ashtrays, biscuit barrels and uniform buttons, and, as on the MS & L before it, water carafes and hotel chamber pots . . . none of them escaped the new insignia. It was to be seen at its best and most lavishly on passenger and goods locomotives, where it was the practice to exhibit it on splashers and tender and tank sides, and on passenger coaches, where it was not unusual to see three adorning each side.

Altogether it was a pleasant design. The winged Pollitt locomotive which forms the crest, and the helmet of Mercury on the centre of the shield, accurately foreshadowed the high speeds of twentieth century Great Central expresses. The upper part of the shield contains parts of the arms of Manchester, Sheffield and Lincoln, side by side, and below them is denoted Leicester, with the hollow cross and short swords representing London. Rather oddly, neither Grimsby nor Nottingham had a look-in. The apt motto *Forward* on the scroll at the base was probably inspired by the famous MS & L Chairman, Sir Edward Watkin, whose South Eastern Railway had earlier adopted *Onward*.

The overall dimensions of this transfer are $12\frac{1}{2}$ in. wide $\times$ $15\frac{1}{4}$ in. high and there was a smaller replica 7 in. wide $\times$ 10 in. high. A more ornate variant, measuring $10\frac{7}{8}$ in. wide $\times$ 15 in. high, was subsequently produced by Tearnes. This embodied red and white mantling with gilt tassels, but the shield was devoid of gilt edging. A locomotive with Robinson characteristics now occupied the crest. It is not known for what purpose this design was used, and there is no evidence that it ever appeared on locomotives or rolling stock.

In 1904 the impoverished and ramshackle Wrexham, Mold & Connahs Quay Railway was vested in the Great Central. Some of its locomotives and coaches displayed a simple garter emblem $9\frac{1}{4}$ in. wide $\times$ $9\frac{3}{4}$ in. high which, because of its great rarity, is reproduced here. It consists of three colours only, gilt and Oxford blue with black shading.

Another railway fell into the Great Central net at the beginning of 1907. This was the Lancashire, Derbyshire & East Coast, for which Tearnes produced early in August 1896 a handsome transfer (Plate 6). It has a diameter of 13 in. and in common with the garter of the Wrexham, Mold & Connahs Quay, is one of the rarest of British railway armorial transfers to survive. The decorative shield is quartered by the arms of Lancaster (top left), originally granted on 6th December 1604, Derby (top right), Nottingham (bottom left) which dates back to 1584 and Lincoln (bottom right) which first appeared fifty years later.

When the Great Central became a constituent company of the LNER it contributed a route mileage of 855 and a well set up fleet of 1,358 locomotives, 2,727 coaching vehicles and 35,330 freight vehicles. Its motto *Forward* was destined to survive for many years on future heraldic designs.

Great Central nickel uniform button (20mm dia)
David Swan Collection

Great Eastern Railway

The Great Eastern was created by an Act of 7th August 1862, which sanctioned the amalgamation of the Eastern Counties, Norfolk, Eastern Union, East Anglian, East Suffolk and other subsidiary undertakings. The Eastern Counties, which was the biggest component, had worked the Norfolk from 1848, the East Anglian from 1852 and the Eastern Union from 1854.

Only two armorial devices of these old railway companies appear to have survived, those of the Eastern Union and Eastern Counties. Some degree of uncertainty is attached to the design of the Eastern Union. It was presented to the Castle Museum, Norwich, by the Great Eastern Railway in 1918, when it was said that it was believed to have been hung originally on the *Bignold Arms* public house, which stood on Eastern Union land near Victoria station, Norwich, the terminus of the line. When the public house was closed down a refreshment room was opened at the station and the device was refixed in the adjacent rotunda until the refreshment room was likewise closed.

The device itself, its motto *Gratitude*, its crest of a red lion *passant reguardant*, holding a gold ear of big-wheat in the dexter forepaw, and its azure shield with two gold ears of big-wheat *in saltire* (crossed diagonally) are derived from those of Bigland, of Bigland Hall, Ulverston, Lancashire and are identical with those of Bignold. Sir Samuel Bignold, a strong advocate of local railway construction, was Deputy Chairman of the Eastern Union for several years, but even so it is rather strange that his device was adopted instead of that of the Chairman, John Chevallier Cobbold, who was the real architect of the company.

Somewhat ostentatious is the design of the Eastern Counties, consisting as it does of six shields spaced around an ancient 2-2-2 locomotive and four-wheeled tender, all of which are framed by masses of ermine. The shield of London takes pride of place at the top, then clockwise follow shields denoting Yarmouth, Norwich, Eye (Suffolk), Colchester and Ipswich.

The Eastern Counties also used the City of London crest, a dragon's wing, as an emblem. An example is illustrated and it will be observed that the cross somewhat unusually follows the shape of the wing. The device was perpetuated by the Great Eastern, who employed it extensively, sometimes with and sometimes without the cross, an example of the latter being depicted in the back of the board-room chair. Elsewhere it was to be seen on the company's stationery, on staff uniform buttons, on some steamship and hotel equipment and on tarpaulins of the Goods Department.

In the bad old days of the 1850s the Eastern Counties became the scape-goat of the railway companies because of its chronic unpunctuality and other shortcomings. George Hoy of Bethnal Green issued a challenge to the directors in 1856 to pit his donkey against some of the business trains. Here was glorious material for contemporary cartoonists, who were not slow to demonstrate their wit. In one cartoon a voice from the Store-keeper's Department asks 'What shall we do with the crest?' The reply of the passengers is to the effect that a fool's cap should be made of it. In its maturity the Great Eastern became efficient and respectable. Out of Liverpool Street it operated the most intensive steam suburban services in the world; it was a pioneer in the use of liquid fuel for locomotives; its main line and Continental services were very good; and its catering was generally superb. To the LNER it handed over 1,191 route miles of line together with 1,343 locomotives, 5,548 coaching vehicles and 30,104 goods and service vehicles.

North Staffordshire final device

North London

Maryport & Carlisle

Wirral

London, Midland & Scottish 1st device

PLATE 5

Manchester, Sheffield & Lincolnshire
1st device (coaches)

Manchester, Sheffield & Lincolnshire
3rd device (locomotives)

Great Central coat of arms

Lancashire, Derbyshire & East Coast

Great Eastern (coaches)

PLATE 6

Eastern Union painted device

Eastern Counties painted device
BRB Collection

The Great Eastern armorial device, which was designed by Henry Parker of the Carriage & Wagon Department at the time of the company's formation, is virtually a geographical guide to the system, although heraldically it is as unorthodox as its predecessor of the Eastern Counties, which basically it resembled.

Eastern Counties painted crest
BRB Collection

London takes the premier place at the hub and above it, at 11 o'clock, is the shield of Middlesex, denoted by the three Saxon seaxes. In heraldry the seax is usually described as a Saxon sword, although in fact it is a stabbing knife with a blade six to eight inches long. The notch on the back (lower edge) of the blade distinguished it from the scimitar, but oddly the incisions did not appear in the Great Eastern device and they were often wrongly omitted on designs used by the county.

Middlesex was once the territory of the Middle Saxons, when it was surrounded by the Kingdoms of the East, West and South Saxons and called Middle-seaxe. For nearly three centuries it was a dependency of the first of these, East-seaxe, and when the strife ended between Alfred the Great and the Danish king of East Anglia it remained Saxon or English territory, whereas East-seaxe (later Essex) was handed over to the Danes. In this way the counties of Middlesex and Essex came to share the same emblem.

Next clockwise from Middlesex is the arms of Maldon, to represent Essex, for at the time the design was evolved Chelmsford had not been incorporated. It may seem strange that the arms of Colchester were not selected, especially as it appears on the Eastern Counties device, but this may have been because of its similarity to the arms of Nottingham which, according to the designer, it was at one time intended to include. In 1862, however, Maldon as a port enjoyed greater prominence than in later years. Furthermore, a close connexion had developed between the town and the railway; David Waddington, Deputy Chairman, and subsequently Chairman of the Eastern Counties, was elected MP for Maldon in 1847.

Representing Suffolk, the next shield carries part of the arms of Ipswich, which had been granted and confirmed by William Harvey, Clarenceux King of Arms, as long ago as 1561. Here again an inexplicable error was committed. The faces of the lions are shown in profile, whereas they should be *guardant*.

Norfolk is represented by the City of Norwich in the fourth shield, a design that was likewise confirmed by William Harvey. It consisted simply of a domed castle above a lion *passant guardant*.

Cambridge follows. The upper part of the shield carries a fleur-de-lis between two roses. Beneath is a bridge with three towers; on the Great Eastern device the towers are charged on the bridge instead of being above it, as on the authorised version. Below the bridge is the river, with three sailing vessels.

The sixth shield simply carries a hart, denoting Hertford, and next to it is the ancient castle of Northampton, supported by two lions *rampant*, again incorrectly in profile, whereas they should be *guardant*. It would be interesting to know why Northampton appeared at all, for there were no Great Eastern lines in the county, let alone the town! The nearest the company's metals got to Northamptonshire was Peterborough, where its station was actually in Huntingdon.

Finally, there is Huntingdon, an excellent example of allusive heraldry. A landscape is depicted, with a tree in the centre, on the lefthand side of which a bird is perched. To the left again is a stag pursued by two hounds. Right of the tree stands a huntsman blowing a horn and holding a bow and arrow. The huntsman represents Robin Hood, reputed Earl of Huntingdon.

The transfer illustrated measures 12 in. wide × 15¼ in. high and embellished coaching stock; there was a smaller version 9 in. wide × 11 in. high with the garter shaded green instead of blue. A replica of the larger transfer, but without the filigree, appeared on most of the passenger tender engines (2-2-2, 4-2-2 and 2-4-0) but when the famous *Claud Hamilton* 4-4-0s appeared a new fashion note was struck. The leading splashers of the engines carried cast metal reproductions 12½ in. wide × 15½ in.

73

high of the company's arms in *bas-relief* and hand enamelled in fu colours. And a brave show these made on the Royal blue livery.

Great Eastern crest on Board Room chair
BRB Collection

Great Northern Railway

The Great Northern was incorporated in 1846 and its first metals fror Louth to Grimsby, leased from the East Lincolnshire, were brought inte use two years later. The first section of its famous main line, destined te become a part of the East Coast Route to Scotland, from a temporar station in Maiden Lane, near Kings Cross, to Peterborough, was openee to the public on 7th August 1850.

Armorial adornment is believed to have made its initial appearance or coaching stock (which throughout the life of the company was given a teak external finish) in 1894 and the transfer produced by Tearnes is the largest the firm made for any British railway. It measures no less than 20¾ in. wide × 27 in. high and is a veritable geographical guide to the system. It is also extremely rare.

At the top of the design is the achievement of the City of London, beneath which is a thistle and rose *motif* to signify the company's Anglo Scottish role. Likewise the upper shield, which is quartered with the

74

lions of England and the lion of Scotland, together with representations of Huntingdon (bottom left) and Peterborough (bottom right), the latter being denoted by the arms of the See alongside those of the Dean of Peterborough, of which the crossed keys and crossed swords are respectively the central features. Below, left, is a shield quartered with part of the arms of Grantham (top left), the full achievements of Nottingham (top right) and Sheffield (bottom left), and part of the arms of Manchester (bottom right). Opposite, is a shield quartered with part of the arms of Doncaster (top left), the full achievement of Leeds (top right), and parts of the arms of York (bottom left) and Bradford (bottom right). Finally, at the base, a small shield bearing a *fleur-de-lis* represents Wakefield!

The inclusion of an approved achievement such as that of the City of London in a design which had never been seen inside the College of Arms got the Great Northern into hot water with that august body when someone brought the *gaffe* to its notice around 1910. In consequence, the company dropped the device like a red hot coal and adopted in its place something much simpler and less informative. The Anglo-Scottish theme now occupied the scene to the exclusion of all else, and henceforward this theme dominated the design of items such as uniform buttons and provided the basis for insignia on official publications.

Two versions of the new transfer, both of which measure $16\frac{1}{2}$ in. wide × 15 in. high, were produced. One, in blue, gold and rust brown, was displayed on some coaching stock; an identical green, gold and rust counterpart was created for the locomotives. Yet only two Great Northern engines, Ivatt's 4-4-0 No 400 of 1896 and the same designer's 4-4-2 No 1442 of 1908, are known to have been armorially embellished. It is very odd that history precisely repeated itself in this way in LNER days.

Great Northern device for coaches
W. H. D. Faulkner Collection

Locomotive No 400 carried a circular device, doubtless hand-painted, on her combined splashers, details of which have not survived. Locomotive No 1442 was given transfers of the final design as if to signify her distinction as the Royal Train engine of the Great Northern. She was unique in that throughout the twenty-five years she ran on the LNER (being numbered 4442 and, finally, 2872) the armorial device of her original owner was carried on the trailing splashers (one of which is preserved in the British Railways Board Collection). No 1442 enjoyed a great reputation for high speed and reliability, a typical instance of which was recorded on 4th June 1916. Working a military special of two corridor coaches at short notice, she covered the 105¼ miles from Kings Cross to Grantham in a fraction over 100 minutes. Apart from a few weeks at Sheffield, she was stationed at Kings Cross throughout a working life of 39 years.

At the end of 1922 the Great Northern handed over to the LNER a system of 1,051¼ route miles and a fleet of 1,359 locomotives, 6 steam rail motors, 3,474 coaching vehicles and 38,706 freight vehicles. It also ensured the enrichment of the future of the new company with its Chief Mechanical Engineer, Herbert Nigel Gresley.

Great Northern gilt uniform button (24mm dia)
David Swan Collection

Great North of Scotland Railway

Farthest north constituent company of the LNER, the Great North of Scotland served the north east corner of the country with a route mileage

Here's a neat monotone reproduction of the iNofS device on "The G N of S Rly 1854-1954" SLS Sept 1954 Vol XXX No 352.

of only 334½, and was known locally as 'The Little and Good'. Like the Great Northern, it was incorporated in 1846; its first section, from Kittybrewster to Huntly, was formally opened on 19th September 1854.

Great North locomotives, of which there were eventually 122, were always painted one shade of green or another until 1914. In that year T. E. Heywood from the Taff Vale took over as Locomotive Superintendent and introduced a black livery with yellow and red lining out, and the leading splashers of the 4-4-0 express engines he eventually built were emblazoned with the company's armorial device.

The latter is a very neat affair and very few specimens have survived. The shield within the garter bearing the name is quartered between the Scottish lion and the castles from the arms of Aberdeen, where the headquarters of the line were situated. The crest is a Scottish lion *séjant* (sitting, or more truthfully in this case, squatting). Overall, the transfer measures 8¾ in. wide × 10 in. high.

So far as the author is aware the company's 766 coaching vehicles, which were finished in lake with cream upper panels, never received any armorial decoration, but a transfer of the company's initials in monogram form embellished each side of the two steam rail motors Nos 29 and 31 built in 1905.

Staff uniform buttons carried a design similar to the locomotive device and an example is illustrated.

Great North of Scotland gilt uniform button (24mm dia)
David Swan Collection

Hull & Barnsley Railway

Time was when the deep rooted dislike and suspicion with which many Hull citizens, inspired by its Corporation, regarded the monopoly of the North Eastern Railway became a byword. Out of this hostile attitude was born the Hull & Barnsley, a comparative late-comer on the railway stage, for it was not incorporated until 1880, when the cumbersome title Hull, Barnsley & West Riding Junction Railway & Dock Company was adopted. Its Alexandra dock was opened on 16th July 1885, its railway for goods traffic on 20th July and for passengers a week later. The western terminus was Cudworth, but Barnsley could be reached from Monk Bretton junction over the metals of the Midland.

Many of the earliest engines, notably the attractive Beyer Peacock 2-4-os and o-6-os of 1885, displayed a monogram of the company's string of initials on the sides of the tenders. The armorial transfer came later, and the basic design of it remained unchanged until the line lost its separate identity.

The device was essentially a gilt and pink bordered *quatrefoil* surrounded by a gilt edged band of umber brown carrying thereon the company's full title in gilt *sans serif* letters shaded black. The four interstices formed by the *quatrefoil* were each occupied by a rose. Within the *quatrefoil* were embraced a winged wheel to denote speedy transport, a shield (left) bearing three ducal coronets to represent Hull, a shield (right) containing *inter alia* shuttles and pickaxes to represent Barnsley and two green tinted dolphins entwined with a gilt trident to denote the company's maritime interests, together with its date of incorporation in gilt. The whole of the background was umber brown.

There were, however, two variants. The first, of date unknown, introduced a Brunswick green field in place of white for the ducal coronets of Hull, but there was no other change. The second followed the adoption of the shorter title on 1st July 1905. Once again Hull's field was altered, this time to middle blue, and some modest gilt leaf-work was added at the foot of the device.

All three designs are 11¾ in. in diameter over black shading but the addition of the ornamental base in the final one increased its height to 13 in. In the last years of the company the transfers appeared on the leading express passenger locomotives and bogie coaching stock, which were given invisible green (black with a green cast in sunlight) and teak finishes respectively.

The Hull & Barnsley was never a prosperous railway and as early as 1887, when already it was heavily in debt, its operation might have been taken over by the Midland, and on more than one subsequent occasion it might have been absorbed by the North Eastern. But not whilst there was a Hull Corporation! Every attempt by the company to associate itself with one of the bigger railways was met by the implacable opposition of the Hull Corporation which, even when the line was to become part of the North Eastern on 1st April 1922, under an amalgamation preliminary to grouping, summoned an abortive public protest meeting.

A fleet of 181 locomotives, 160 coaching vehicles and 4,808 freight vehicles, and a route mileage of 106½ passed to the North Eastern, but following the precedent set elsewhere for the Lancashire & Yorkshire, the Hull & Barnsley was always regarded as a constituent company of the LNER and, indeed, had a Director appointed to its Board.

Hull & Barnsley 1st device
W. H. D. Faulkner Collection

Hull & Barnsley 2nd device

North British Railway

See supplement p.16

The first railway to cross the border between Scotland and England was the North British, incorporated in 1844. Its main line from Edinburgh to Berwick and branch from Longniddry to Haddington were opened to the public on 22nd June 1846.

This was the modest beginning of the largest of the pregrouping Scottish railway companies. At the end of its independent existence it reached Glasgow in the west, Fort Augustus and Mallaig in the north west, Stirling, Perth and Dundee in the north and Bervie and Kinnaber junction in the north east. From the last named it enjoyed running powers over the metals of its eternal rival, the Caledonian, into Aberdeen. Berwick in the south east and Carlisle and Silloth in the south west were its other extremities and between these points it penetrated England to Rothbury, Hexham and Morpeth. Altogether it owned, leased or worked 1,378 route miles of track and possessed 1,075 locomotives, 3,576 coaching vehicles and 55,806 freight vehicles.

The NB, as it was popularly known, had several claims to fame. Within its system were the famous Forth and Tay bridges, and Waverley station in Edinburgh was (and still is) the largest Scottish railway station. In 1871 it became the first to introduce the ubiquitous 4-4-0 locomotive with inside frames throughout and inside cylinders. Two years later it pioneered the British sleeping car and, in 1913, installed the first Scottish train control, based on Portobello. And in 1919 its new 12-wheeled dining cars were amongst the first, if not the first, examples of steel passenger rolling stock in Great Britain.

Despite the numerous amalgamations and take-overs of the years of growth the NB never changed its heraldic device which, framed by a *motif* of roses and thistles, contained the arms of Edinburgh and Berwick, the places at the ends of its original main line. The city arms of Edinburgh, which is represented by the castle there, were registered in 1732. Supporters are a maiden and a hind, and in the NB device these are embodied in the shield.

Edinburgh & Glasgow painted device
Metro-Cammell Ltd Collection

The transfer measures 11⅝ in. wide × 13½ in. high and very well it looked on the bronze green passenger tender and tank engines and the dark crimson coaches. There was a variant in which a plain garter, without buckle or any other ornamentation, took the place of the ornamental one illustrated; it is not known for what purpose it was employed. A plain circular transfer carrying the company's name, measuring 11¾ in. in diameter, is reproduced. This, it is surmised, was displayed on rolling stock of the Edinburgh, Perth & Dundee Railway, which dated back to 1849 and was incorporated in the North British in 1862, the year shown on the transfer. No doubt the vehicle number was inserted within it.

Of the other railways absorbed by the North British one of the most important was the Edinburgh & Glasgow, which had been incorporated in 1838. Its armorial device and two monograms are reproduced. The first named, it will be seen, exhibits the crest of Edinburgh, an anchor, and the shield is quartered by the arms of Edinburgh and Glasgow. The motto surrounding the left hand monogram *Nisi dominus frustra—Unless God be with us all is in vain*—is that of Edinburgh.

North British garter
W. H. D. Faulkner Collection

North Eastern Railway

See supplement p. 7

Largest and financially strongest constituent company of the LNER was the North Eastern, created by Act of 31st July 1854. The Act dissolved the York & North Midland and Leeds Northern Railways and vested their undertakings in the York, Newcastle & Berwick, at the same time embracing the change of name of the latter to *North Eastern*. It also contained clauses for the protection of the Hull & Selby, whose lease in perpetuity by the York & North Midland was in process of settlement.

The York & North Midland was the oldest of the three, having been incorporated in 1836. This was the line on which George Hudson, its first Chairman and the first of our 'Railway Kings', began his meteoric rise and fall as an entrepreneur whose aim was to create a national railway system under his *aegis*. The first section of the Y & NM, from York to South Milford, was opened with much ceremony on 29th May 1839. And by the time it became part of the North Eastern it had grown by extension and purchase to a system bounded in the north by and including the Leeds–Scarborough line and in the south by the river Humber.

For its coat of arms the Y & NM practically adopted the arms of the city of York, of which Thomas Allen, in his *History of York* had the following interesting observations to make:

'The arms of the city of York are of great antiquity. Prior to the reign of William I they were simply *argent* (silver) a cross *gules* (red). The five lions *or* (gold) with which the cross is now charged, it is said, were added by the Conqueror in memory of five heroic magistrates viz. Sir Robert Clifford, Howngate, Talbot, Lacells and Erringham, who had bravely defended the city against him, till famine obliged them to submit.'

Hand-painted specimens of the Y & NM device, one of which is reproduced, embody a red cross on a white field. On some of its dark green coaches the company also displayed hand-painted monograms of its initials, a rare example of which is illustrated.

York & North Midland painted monogram
Metro-Cammell Ltd Collection

The York, Newcastle & Berwick was itself a product of amalgamation, dating back to 1847, when the merger of the York & Newcastle with the

Newcastle & Berwick took place. The first named of these had been formed in 1842 as the Newcastle & Darlington Junction, changing its name to *York & Newcastle* four years later when it purchased the Great North of England, which had been opened for passenger traffic between Darlington and York on 30th March 1841 and which emblazoned its coaches with the arms of York, Durham and Newcastle.

It will be seen that the hand-painted device of the YN & B embraced parts of the arms of the three places in its title. Three castellated towers are carried by the red shield of Newcastle. Little appears to be known about this design, which is a very old one, but it is believed that one of the towers may represent the 'new' castle erected by Robert, eldest son of William I; another was built on the site by Henry II. A little more is recorded of the Berwick device. In *The Arms of the Royal and Parliamentary Burghs of Scotland* by the Marquis of Bute it was said:

'The arms appear to be *argent*, on a mount or bear *statant* before an oak tree, all proper . . . the bear being a pun upon Berwick. The device . . . consists of two shields bearing France (modern) and England quarterly, that on the *sinister* ensigned with a label, the two coats being thus the arms of the King of England and of the Prince of Wales, and at the top a robed and seated figure having the right hand raised in benediction and the left holding an orb surmounted by a cross, doubtless intended to represent Christ.'

A different theme was followed by the Leeds Northern, which was incorporated as the Leeds & Thirsk in 1845, the first portion of which was opened for goods and mineral traffic between Thirsk and Ripon on 5th January 1848. The Leeds & Thirsk adopted a cast metal replica of its seal, excluding only the year of incorporation and adding typical contemporary external ornamentation, for the adornment of its first class carriages. This, it will be observed, consists of a shield divided into three parts and displaying a sheaf of corn (top left) to indicate the agricultural interests of the line, a fleece (top right) taken from the arms of Leeds and (below) a fish closely resembling a trout, doubtless to remind anglers that there was a noted trout stream in the neighbourhood of Thirsk. The device measures 12 in. wide × 14¼ in. high overall.

When the title *Leeds Northern* was assumed on 9th August 1851 alterations were made to the new seal and, once again, a replica of it was introduced for the emblazoning of the first class carriages. The shield was now divided into the customary four quarters, the three mullets and a fleece denoting Leeds, the sailing ship depicting the maritime association arising from the company's connexion with the West Hartlepool Harbour & Railway, and the three bales of wool and three sheaves of corn the principal traffic of the line.

York & North Midland painted device

York, Newcastle & Berwick painted device

Leeds & Thirsk in metal

Leeds Northern painted device

Leeds was destined to appear on the two devices of the North Eastern and, as shown in earlier pages, it is to be seen on those of the Manchester & Leeds, the North Midland, the Midland and the Great Northern. But only in the case of the last named was the full achievement embodied. The three mullets (rowels of spurs) across the upper part of the shield are taken from the arms of the Danby family, one of whom was the first Mayor, and the heraldic golden fleece, which is a sheep supported from a belt, underlines the prosperity which the woollen industry has brought to Leeds. The crest and supporters are owls, and here again there is allusion to a family association; the heraldry of the Savile family contains owls, and Sir John Savile was the first Alderman. The motto *Pro rege et lege* at the base of the design means *For king and the law*.

From the York & North Midland the North Eastern inherited a lease of the Hull & Selby. This short but important line had been incorporated in 1836 and was opened throughout on 1st July 1840. Prior to its lease exactly five years later it had devised for itself an extremely opulent looking emblem which embodied the arms of Selby Abbey (left) and Hull (right). It is believed that this was painted on the sides of some of the coaches, which were given a dark green livery. The Hull & Selby was purchased by the North Eastern in 1872, having retained until that date its position as a leased company.

Another railway based on Hull to fall in to the North Eastern net was the little Hull & Holderness, which had been incorporated in 1853 and opened between Hull and Withernsea on 24th July of the following year. By some miracle two different hand painted versions of its armorial device have been preserved and both are illustrated. The three ducal coronets of Hull form the crest and the shield is quartered by a 2-2-2 locomotive, two sheaves of corn, a young bull and a ship, all denoting the interests of the line. And what an extraordinary contraption is that locomotive, with splashers to all its wheels, an engorged smokebox and boiler mountings smacking of a condiment set! It will be noticed, too, that there are considerable differences between the two ships. In one design it is three-masted with a decided rake to the funnel; in the other it is two-masted, with sails unfurled, and the funnel stands primly erect behind a paddle box.

The Hull & Holderness was worked by the North Eastern from the beginning of 1860 and taken over two years later.

In the same year the important Newcastle & Carlisle was amalgamated with the North Eastern. This railway had been incorporated in 1829 and its first section, between Blaydon and Hexham, was brought into use for goods traffic in 1834. It was ceremonially opened throughout on 18th June—Waterloo Day—1838 and for a brief period at the end of the 1840s was

Hull & Holderness painted device
BRB Collection

Hull & Holderness painted device variant
BRB Collection

Great North of Scotland

Hull & Barnsley final device

Great Northern 1st device (coaches)

PLATE 7

North Eastern (coaches)

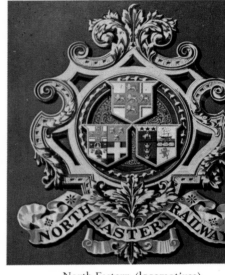

North Eastern (locomotives)

Londonderry, Seaham & Sunderland

PLATE 8

Hull & Selby painted device
BRB Collection

Newcastle & Carlisle painted device
BRB Collection

leased to the York, Newcastle & Berwick. Apart from that interlude it maintained an independent existence until 17th June 1862 when, on the third attempt before Parliament, its union with the North Eastern was authorised.

A most attractive armorial device adorned the outer compartment door panels of the yellow first class coaches. An ornamental shield embracing the arms of Newcastle (left) and Carlisle (right) occupies the centre of the design; its crest is that of Newcastle, a castellated tower on a wreath and carrying a demi-lion which bears a forked pennant; and its supporters also those of Newcastle, are two superb seahorses.

The year 1862 saw the North Eastern spheres of influence extended from Saltburn to Tebay and Penrith and from Barnard Castle to Consett. This was brought about by the absorption of the historic Stockton & Darlington Railway on 28th July, a line which from humble beginning had grown into a system of 200 miles and was known all over the world. It had been incorporated in 1821 and its opening on 27th September 1824 heralded the dawn of steam traction on public railways. But its seal depicted a horse pulling wagons! It never indulged in an heraldic device but it did, however, display its coach numbers within hand-painted garters and one of them is illustrated, together with a contemporary North Eastern specimen.

Stockton & Darlington garter for coaches   North Eastern garter for coaches

Discounting the take over of the Hull & Barnsley, which was really a preliminary step in the grouping of railways, the last acquisition of note by the North Eastern was the Londonderry, Seaham & Sunderland, which occurred on 6th October 1900. This was some 7 miles in length and had been opened on 3rd August 1854, having been built by its owner, the Marquis of Londonderry, to secure a direct connexion between his collieries and a port of shipment.

The Londonderry, as it was usually called, owned 2,863 freight vehicles, but it also ran passenger services and could boast 22 coaching vehicles, which were given a lake finish. The coaches, and some of the 13 green liveried locomotives which completed the fleet, were embellished with the neat coronet design illustrated. This measures $9\frac{3}{4}$ in. wide $\times$ $12\frac{1}{2}$ in. high and is another extremely rare transfer.

Two quite different armorial transfer designs were produced for the North Eastern. The older and smaller of the two is circular, having an overall width of $11\frac{1}{2}$ in. and height of $12\frac{1}{4}$ in., within which the company's title surrounds three shields representing the original constituent railways, York & North Midland (top) Leeds Northern (bottom left) and York, Newcastle & Berwick (bottom right), the arrangement being identical with that of the seal of the last named; thus it is an historical rather than a geographical design. It was introduced for the ornamentation of the grass green locomotives and crimson lake coaching stock alike and, it is believed, was first to be seen on the latter. Its first appearance on the locomotives can, however, be established as 1888, for it was worn by T. W. Worsdell's initial class I 4-2-2 of that year. Hitherto North Eastern passenger engines had carried the letters *NER* on tender and tank sides. Now these were replaced by the words *North* and *Eastern*, with the armorial transfer centred between them. The large single splashers were also each adorned with the transfer.

This circular design was the company's standard emblem and remained in use until the end of 1922. It was to be seen on stationery on official publications and in other places, being reproduced in *full colour* even on the sides of hotel chamber pots.

In 1896 the second design was ordered. Its display was always confined to locomotives, so far as the author is aware, and although it made its *début* on the single splashers of rebuilt class I 4-2-2 engines, its customary position was between the words *North* and *Eastern* on tender and tank sides, thus displacing the circular emblem. Henceforth, the latter was restricted to splashers, as a general rule, where locomotives were concerned, but there were a few exceptions for a time. In the case of express passenger locomotives, therefore, the unusual practice grew up of decorating one or perhaps two pairs of the splashers with transfers of the first design and each tender side with transfers of the second design. The handsome class T 0-8-0 mineral engines carried the earlier design on the large sandbox over the third pair of coupled wheels.

The second design, much the largest of the two, measures $15\frac{1}{2}$ in. wide × $18\frac{3}{4}$ in. high and flaunts more exuberant ornamentation than heraldry. It will be observed that the three shields are exhibited vertically, with the York & North Midland arms still at the apex, but the two others are transposed. Some of the components have also been changed, only those of the York & North Midland shield remaining unaltered. The York, Newcastle & Berwick shield displays the gold cross of Durham on a blue ground in the fourth quarter in place of the second representation of York. And the Leeds Northern shield retains Leeds and a three-masted ship in the first and second quarters but embodies the three ducal coronets of Hull and the three three-masted ships and *rampant* lion of Middlesbrough in the third and fourth respectively. The second design, like the first, remained in use until the end of 1922.

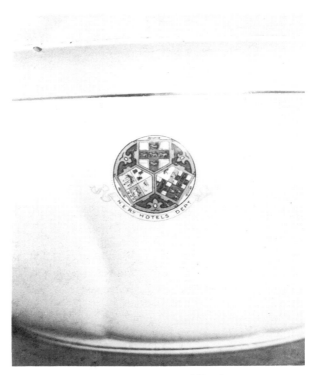

Chamber pot device in full colours

By that time the North Eastern had become the fourth longest railway in the British Isles. It was the largest dock-owning company and handled a heavier tonnage of mineral and coal traffic than any other line. Even without the Hull & Barnsley contribution it could muster 2,013 steam locomotives and 12 electric locomotives, 2 petrol rail motors, 70 electric motor cars and 55 trailer cars, together with 4,116 coaching vehicles and 123,723 freight vehicles. Inevitably it became the senior partner in the new company.

Colne Valley & Halstead Railway

Only three of the twenty-six subsidiary companies which were assigned to the LNER possessed any locomotives and rolling stock of their own. They were the Colne Valley & Halstead, the East & West Yorkshire Union and the Mid-Suffolk Light Railways. Of these, only the first named embellished its passenger rolling stock and some of its locomotives with an armorial device.

Incorporated in 1856, the first section of the Colne Valley & Halstead Railway was opened four years later. It ran through delightful Essex countryside from Chappel & Wakes Colne, on the Great Eastern's Marks Tey–Bury St Edmunds line, to Haverhill in Suffolk, on the same company's Cambridge–Long Melford line, a distance of 19 miles. It owned 5 locomotives, 14 coaching vehicles and 174 freight vehicles. The locomotive livery was black and the coach livery dun brown, varnished teak making an appearance in 1906 when an experimental three-car multiple unit set was bought second-hand from the Metropolitan District Railway; converted into a smart rake of two third class coaches and a composite brake, they were the only bogie vehicles the line possessed.

The company's heraldic transfer is illustrated. This consists simply of three shields denoting Essex (top), Halstead (left) and Haverhill (right) above the year of incorporation in gilt, encircled by an apple green garter with gilt edging, ornamentation and lettering, the latter outlined in black. It measures 10 in. wide × 10½ in. high.

Only a few of these were needed to meet the company's requirements and, coupled with the complete destruction by Allied bombers of the Nuremburg works of the German suppliers during the last war, the Colne Valley & Halstead transfer is, in consequence, one of the most difficult of all for collectors to obtain.

London & North Eastern 1st totem

London & North Eastern Railway

With the North Eastern Railway dominating the Eastern, North Eastern and East Scottish group of companies the assumption of a title such as *London & North Eastern Railway* was almost inevitable. Unfortunately, it paid no regard to lines owned in Denbighshire, Flintshire, the Wirral, Lancashire, Carlisle, Glasgow and the West Highlands. How much simpler and more appropriate would have been *Northern Railway* or, as the designate Chairman, William Whitelaw suggested, *Great North Railway*. But Whitelaw was up against certain North Eastern directors who were determined to have their own way.

For a few months the ugly abbreviation *L & NER* began to appear on the sides of locomotives and coaches, in some cases made more unpleasant by the addition of full points after each initial. Fortunately, W. M. Teasdale, an ex-North Eastern man who became the company's first Advertising Manager, got off to a good start with the universal use of the more euphonious and easier-on-the-eye *LNER* for timetables, posters, press advertisements and booklets, and this was soon adopted for locomotives and rolling stock save only freight vehicles, which were lettered *NE*.

A totem was evolved as early as 1923 for timetable covers, handbills and posters. This is exemplified on the white cover of the Great Eastern section 3d. timetables of 1st October of that year. White was soon replaced by startling tangerine, and Gayton *serif* lettering, including that of the company's full title inside the totem, became the standard for timetable covers.

In 1924 the LNER emulated the Great Central by obtaining a grant of arms. This was one of the most beautiful of all railway heraldic devices and it is indeed regrettable that no transfer of it was ever made. Bounding through clouds of steam, Mercury, whose winged helmet has been noted on the Great Central device, made an apt crest and, as subsequent events proved, a harbinger of the superb high speed performances which steam locomotives were to attain on LNER metals. The shield was divided by St George's cross of London, which bore the four lions of York with the castle of Edinburgh at the centre. The Anglo-Scottish character of the company was emphasised by the display of two London griffins, a rose and a thistle in the four quarters, whilst two magnificent lions, one wearing a collar of roses and the other a collar of thistles, acted as supporters. The fitting motto *Forward* was, of course, inherited from the Great Central coat of arms.

This attractive achievement was hand-painted in full colours on the cab sides of Pacific No. 4472 *Flying Scotsman* which was displayed at the

London & North Eastern gilt uniform button (23mm dia)
David Swan Collection

Arms on LNER Medal

Wembley Exhibition in 1924 and 1925; it was removed in 1928 and restored when the engine passed to the private ownership of Alan Pegler. In 1944 former Great Northern 4-4-0 No. 2000 was reserved for the haulage of directors' and officers' specials. Considerably smartened-up, the tender sides were embellished with the LNER coat of arms, hand-painted again, of course, but the offside crest depicted Mercury speeding from left to right, so as to face the leading end of the engine . . . a silly alteration to make. So history repeated itself, only two LNER locomotives bearing the company's armorial device, as in the case of the Great Northern before it.

Gill totem and lettering for station fascia

The coat of arms never ornamented any units of the teak finished passenger rolling stock, so far as the author is aware, but it appeared in full on prestige publications and, without crest and supporters, on staff uniform buttons, on higher grade stationery and on one side of the LNER medal. Amongst unexpected places where it was to be seen was in Dutch tiles in ss *Arnhem*, the last steamship to be built by the company for the Harwich–Hook of Holland service.

In 1928 Teasdale became an Assistant General Manager and C. G. G. Dandridge, an ex-Great Central man, followed him as Advertising

Manager to initiate a vast programme of typographical reform. Gill Sans, a noble *sans serif* alphabet devised by Eric Gill, the famous sculptor and type designer, was adopted as the standard typeface for posters, handbills and press advertisements with immensely beneficial results. Its employment for station and other signs soon followed, and before the outbreak of war in 1939 it had made its appearance on locomotives, rolling stock and road vehicles.

Gill designed a simple and attractive totem which replaced the earlier example on timetable covers and which was embodied to great advantage in the fascias of modernised stations. Eventually it embellished the sides of the blue and Quaker grey cars of the Tyneside electric lines and the bunkers of a batch of 0-8-0 tank engines rebuilt from former Great Central 0-8-0 tender engines during the last war.

After the demise of the LNER at nationalisation the outline of Gill's totem was appropriated by Jacobs, the biscuit manufacturers, for the adornment of their motor delivery vans, where it is still to be seen today.

Eric Gill's totem

PART THREE

Great Western Railway
and Predecessors

Alexandra (Newport & South Wales) Docks & Railway

With only 38 locomotives, 4 coaches, 677 freight vehicles and $9\frac{1}{4}$ route miles of track of its own it would appear, on the face of it, extraordinary that this little railway could claim to be a constituent company of the Great Western when grouping took place under the Act of 1921. The reason was, of course, that the company was also the owner of an enormous dock estate with 108 miles of sidings.

Alexandra (N&SW) Docks & Railway garter monogram
BRB Collection

The undertaking dated back to 1865, when the Alexandra (Newport) Dock Company was created; the unwieldy title *Alexandra (Newport & South Wales) Docks & Railway* was assumed seventeen years later. In 1897 the Pontypridd, Caerphilly & Newport Railway, built in the early 1880s for bringing coal from the Rhondda and Aberdare valleys to Newport for shipment, was absorbed. It consisted of two separate sections connected by other railways, namely from PC & N junction, at Pontypridd, to Penrhos junction, outside Caerphilly, and from Bassaleg to Mendalgyf junction on the Alexandra Railway at Newport. An Alexandra train running between Pontypridd and Newport thus travelled over the metals of the Taff Vale, the Rhymney and the Brecon & Merthyr Railways as well as its own.

No heraldic device was adopted by the company, but a transfer 12½ in. wide × 14 in. high was made of its initials in the form of a monogram, the display of which appears to have been somewhat limited. Like that of the Liverpool Overhead, the initials are multi-coloured: red A, blue-grey N, green D, gilt & and gilt R. The initials S and W were omitted, perhaps on grounds of overcrowding!

Barry Railway

One of the best, if not the best, of the leading Welsh railways was the Barry, which from the outset was planned as an integrated dock and railway undertaking by the coalowners and shipping interests who were its principal backers. It was also the youngest, having been incorporated as late as 1884 as the Barry Dock & Railways Company; the name was changed to *Barry Railway Company* seven years later.

The first section of line authorised was from Barry to Cadoxton and thence to the Taff Vale Railway at Trehafod junction, beyond Pontypridd, together with four short branches. In the event, the Barry–Cogan section, sanctioned later, was the first to be opened with a local passenger service which started on 20th December 1888. The ceremonial opening of the dock and main line took place on 18th July of the following year; with its 73 acres the dock made all the others at South Wales ports look rather small beer.

Barry trains eventually reached Cardiff over the metals of the Taff Vale and Great Western, Rhymney over those of the Brecon & Merthyr and Coity over those of the Vale of Glamorgan (which it always worked). Although it operated less than 68 route miles of line, its total length of single track, including sidings, exceeded 300 miles and it coped efficiently with an annual traffic of 10 million tons or more through Barry dock.

D. S. M. Barrie, author of the Oakwood Press history of the line, has recorded that many of its well proportioned, twin-gabled station buildings were ornamented with the initials *BR* on one gable and the date on the other. A monogram of the initials *BR*, encircled by a garter bearing the title of the company, was the first transfer produced in 1892, for the decoration of locomotives and passenger rolling stock alike; it was also to be seen on the sides of the brown mineral brake vans, the only British example known to the author of such adornment of freight rolling stock. It measures 11⅝ in. wide × 14 in. high over black shading; the garter is middle green with gilt edging and embellishments and carries black shaded gilt lettering; the monogram is gilt on a transparent background. Amongst garter transfers it is a great rarity.

The armorial transfer of the Barry, 12¼ in. wide × 12¾ in. high over black shading, and printed in 1904, looked well on the crimson lake locomotives and coaches. The red Welsh dragon *passant*, wings *addorsed* (back to back) is surmounted by a stag *at gaze* as crest, this latter being taken from the arms of the Windsor-Clives. Lord Windsor, created Earl of Plymouth in 1905, held the chairmanship of the Barry throughout its corporate life.

When it ended, its legacy to the Great Western included a well maintained fleet of 148 locomotives, 194 coaching vehicles and 1,383 freight vehicles, and a reputation for splendid dividends. During its last decade it never paid less than 9½ per cent on its Ordinary Stock!

Barry garter monogram

Barry gilt uniform button (23mm dia)
David Swan Collection

Cambrian Railways

The longest Welsh railway, but by no means the busiest, for it served no industrial squalor, was the Cambrian. It was created in 1864 by the amalgamation of four little railways, the Llanidloes & Newtown, the Newtown & Machynlleth, the Oswestry & Newtown and the Oswestry, Ellesmere & Whitchurch. The main line they formed was extended from Machynlleth to Aberystwyth and to Pwllheli by the Aberystwyth & Welsh Coast, which entered the Cambrian fold under an Act of 1865, two years before it was opened. Southwards from Llanidloes the Mid-Wales Railway built a line to the Brecon & Merthyr at Talyllyn, opened in 1864; the Cambrian took over the operation of the Mid-Wales in 1888 and absorbed it in 1904. These railways constituted the main framework of the Cambrian, which eventually owned a route mileage of 241¼ and leased or worked a further 57.

Heraldically, the Cambrian was the most interesting of all the Welsh railways. Yet the three histories inspired by its chequered career, by Gasquoine in 1922, Kidner in 1954, and Christiansen and Miller in 1967-68, are remarkably silent on the subject. Gasquoine does, however, go so far as to observe that the Cambrian armorial device, which he mistakenly calls a crest, was originally designed and presented to the directors by W. W. E. Wynne, a noted antiquarian of Peniarth, Towyn, but he does not say which design.

Both the seal and armorial device of the company consisted basically of a shield shared by a Welsh dragon and an English rose to denote the extent of its territory. The oldest and largest examples of the arms are doubtless those to be seen in the brickwork of two gable ends of Frankton station, which was brought into use in 1866 and closed some one hundred years later.

The earliest armorial transfers were based upon the Frankton design. There were two versions, both produced by Tearnes, but the dates they appeared have not survived. In the first, it is believed, when the lower panels of the coaching stock were finished dark brown, the circlet bearing the title and date of incorporation was pink; in the later, when dark brown had given way to bronze green, the circlet was coloured grass green. In all other respects, both as regards design and colouring, the two versions are identical, each having a diameter of 8⅝ in.

Unaccountable lapses, it will be noticed, occurred in all these designs. The company's title is wrongly shown in the singular and the Welsh emblem looks much more like a domestic fowl on the rampage than a dragon! The latter is particularly noticeable in both transfers.

However, all was put right in the third transfer design. The dragon, still green, appeared on a white instead of a gold field and really looked like a dragon; the rose, now formalised, was also given a white instead of a maroon field; and the white shaded blue letters *C R Co* within the *trefoil*

Cambrian in brickwork at Frankton station

Cambrian 1st device
W. H. D. Faulkner Collection

Cambrian 2nd device
W. H. D. Faulkner Collection

had gone, giving an altogether tidier effect. In no other respects were there any alterations in design or colour and the diameter remained at $8\frac{5}{8}$ in.

The Cambrian adopted the Prince of Wales' feathers as its crest. It was worn as a badge on the caps and buttons of the uniformed staff and was painted or stencilled in white on the sides of some of the freight rolling stock. Tearnes produced it in transfer form, in three sizes, of which the example illustrated, which measures 8 in. wide × 7 in. high, was most frequently used on locomotives, carriages, buses and horsedrawn vans, generally in company with the arms but sometimes alone.

Cambrian crest

See Supplement p.8 When the Mid-Wales Railway was taken over 38 coaches were acquired. Their livery was brick red and some of them at least were adorned with the company's armorial transfer which consisted simply of the title surrounding a mounted warrior in the act of slaying a dragon—not a Welsh one, needless to say! It has not been possible to discover the significance of the design. The transfer has an overall diameter of $9\frac{1}{8}$ in. and is one of the most unusual as well as one of the most rare of all British railway devices.

Within the Cambrian empire were two narrow gauge lines which both began as independent companies and which miraculously have survived. First to be opened was the 1 ft. $11\frac{1}{2}$ in. gauge Vale of Rheidol Light Railway, which was brought into use between Aberystwyth and Devil's Bridge in 1902 and absorbed by the Cambrian in 1913. During the early years of its independence it displayed on its coaching stock a distinctive circular transfer of $10\frac{1}{2}$ in. in diameter, the pictorial part of which gives a view of Devil's Bridge. Its three attractive little engines working the line

North British

London & North Eastern painted coat of arms

Colne Valley & Halstead

PLATE 9

Barry

Cambrian final device

Mid-Wales

Vale of Rheidol

PLATE 10

today are unique in two respects; they are the only steam locomotives in active service now owned by British Railways and they are also the only steam locomotives ever to wear the latest blue livery.

The other line was the 2 ft. 6 in. gauge Welshpool & Llanfair Light Railway which was opened between Welshpool and Llanfair Caereinion in 1903 and worked by the Cambrian from the start. Although it retained its independence until grouping, when it was treated as a subsidiary company of the Great Western, its locomotives and rolling stock wore the Cambrian livery until 1923, the handsome bogie coaches carrying a monogram of the owning company. Passenger traffic ceased early in 1931 but the operation of goods traffic went on for another twenty-five years, the last train being run on 3rd November 1956, a special organised by the Stephenson Locomotive Society.

Thanks to the activities of enthusiasts, energetic steps were taken to resurrect the line and it was leased to the Welshpool & Llanfair Light Railway Preservation Company on Christmas Day 1962. A year later a section was reopened on a seasonal basis. A livery of crimson red has been adopted for the now variegated passenger coaches and a garter transfer reproducing the old initials in their original form has made its appearance. This consists of an 8½ in. diameter circlet of grass green, edged and lettered in gold, shaded black and red, the initials being displayed in white on a black background. And very effective it looks, too.

Welshpool & Llanfair Light Railway Preservation Co

Cardiff Railway

Many British ports owe their existence and prosperity to railway enter-prise. In the case of Bute Docks and the Cardiff Railway the reverse applied

—the railway was built to facilitate the movement of traffic to and from the docks. This took place after a bitter Parliamentary battle against opponents which were headed by the Taff Vale Railway. In 1897 the Bute Docks Company was empowered to change its name to *Cardiff Railway Company* and to construct five new lines. These included a main line from Heath junction, on the Rhymney, to the vicinity of Treforest on the Taff Vale; between Cardiff and Heath junction it enjoyed running powers over the Rhymney.

Although the mileage sanctioned exceeded 24 only 11½ were built and the connexion near Treforest was never brought into use for regular traffic. A passenger service with steam rail motors was started in 1911.

The heraldic device of the company was a simple one consisting of the old Cardiff arms (left) and part of the arms of the Marquess of Bute dividing the motto *Wrth Ddwr a Than—By water and fire* as if to perpetuate the memory of the tribulations which attended the birth of its railway! The transfer measures 10½ in. in diameter and originated in 1891.

At the end of its existence the Cardiff possessed only 36 locomotives, 8 passenger train vehicles and 43 goods train vehicles. But it was as a dock owner that it ranked as a constituent company of the Great Western, with a contribution of five docks totalling 165 acres served by 120 miles of railway.

Rhymney Railway

See Supplement p. 5

Although the Rhymney Railway terminated hard by Bute East dock at Cardiff it was not a dock owning company; its life blood was the shipment of coal from the Rhymney and other valleys. It was incorporated in 1854 to build a main line from a point near the Rhymney Iron Works to a junction at Hengoed with the Newport, Abergavenny & Hereford Railway. Authority to extend southwards to the Taff Vale Railway at Walnut Tree Bridge junction, Taffs Well, was secured in the following year. From this point running powers were to be exercised to Crockherbtown junction, Cardiff, whence Rhymney metals would be resumed to Bute East dock. This last section was the first to be opened, in 1857, the remainder being brought into use in the following year.

Dependence upon the Taff Vale ceased in 1871, when the Rhymney opened its own direct road from Caerphilly via Llanishen to its dock branch at Cardiff. Eventually the company's route mileage totalled 40 and its share of short joint lines, two with the Great Western and one with the North Western, was 11. It owned 123 locomotives, which wore Brunswick green, with frames finished in chocolate, 131 coaching vehicles and 1,046 freight vehicles.

there is a b&w illustration of the
Cardiff Rly device in
"Great Western Rly"   J N Slinn   213

A pure circular form favoured by several Welsh lines was adopted for its armorial emblem and the colourful transfer manufactured by Tearnes has a diameter of 9½ in. Its components in the upper part within the title depict a furnace of a type introduced at Rhymney Iron Works in the 1820s and a three-masted sailing ship. Beneath are shields from the arms of Cardiff (left) and Newport (right).

Why the chevrons of Cardiff are shown white instead of the correct gold is not known. And why the inclusion of Newport, which the Rhymney never reached? The reasoning advanced by D. S. M. Barrie, in his Oakwood Press history of the line, seems to afford the most likely explanation. He recalled that the Rhymney and the Newport, Abergavenny & Hereford were allied in the formative years and both in the prospectus and in the preamble to the Act of Incorporation there were references to the '*ports of the Bristol Channel*'. And that the rejected Rhymney Railway (New Lines) Bill of 1861 sought to give the company running powers over 'the Newport section or railway of the West Midland company.'

In 1907 Tearnes produced a variant of the armorial transfer which embodied an outer red band, thus increasing the diameter to 12 in., and *gold* chevrons in the Cardiff arms. The use to which it was put is not known.

Early Taff Vale garter and crest
W. H. D. Faulkner Collection

Taff Vale Railway

The earliest armorial device of the Taff Vale Railway was formed of the Prince of Wales' feathers and the motto *Ich Dien* embraced within a circlet carrying the full title of the company. It is a pity that no specimen appears to have survived as it must afford the first instance of this particular Royal cipher being adapted for railway purposes. The Taff Vale was one of the oldest Welsh lines; incorporated on 21st June 1836, it was the first public railway of any real magnitude in the Principality. It was also destined to be the only South Wales system with any significant stretch of quadruple track; of its ultimate route mileage of 124½ owned, leased or worked, over 22 were four-tracked, including 12 miles of its main line between Pontypridd and Cardiff.

On 9th October 1840 the first section was brought into public use between Abercynon (then Navigation House) and Cardiff. On 12th April of the following year the main line was opened throughout with the completion of the section from Abercynon northwards to Merthyr. Thereafter the company's metals were extended both by amalgamation and by the construction of new lines, some of the latter being of a defensive nature as other railways developed on the flanks, eager to share in the traffic bonanza the iron and coal industries in the area had to offer. Eventually, Taff Vale trains were to be seen in Aberdare, Maerdy, Treherbert, Llantrisant, Aberthaw and Penarth, amongst other places.

Despite the inroads of competitors, of which those of the Barry made the greatest impact, the Taff Vale carried not far short of 8 million tons of originating coal, coke and other minerals in its final year. Like some of its neighbours, its freight vehicle stock of 2,372 in no way reflected the immense tonnages moved annually because the vast bulk was conveyed in privately owned wagons. The Taff Vale also enjoyed an originating traffic of some 8 million passengers, for which it ran a fleet of 408 coaching vehicles and 4 steam rail motors. Its stock of locomotives totalled 271, the 0-6-2 tanks outnumbering the rest by more than three to one.

The first transfer for the line was the gartered crest illustrated. It measures 7⅞ in. wide × 9⅞ in. high and introduced the goat, as a crest, and the motto *Cymru a fu a chymru a fydd*—*Wales hath been and Wales shall be* which became features of the armorial transfers of later years. The goat is in natural colours and the garter lettering is gilt on a background of Oxford blue. The use to which the emblem was put is not known, but it was most likely a coach adornment.

Two armorial transfers, basically of the same design, were displayed simultaneously by the Taff Vale. The smaller, which measures 7⅞ in. wide × 12⅞ in. high over black shading, embodies a circular garter and

Taff Vale – see ref in Hamilton
Ellis "The Trains we Loved" pp
63/4

Port Talbot Rly & Docks Co.

   See "Great Western Way" by J N Slinn p 253
   – Is the cap anything to do with Marquess of Bute?

was to be seen on most of the coaching stock, which was given an external finish of dark chocolate with white upper panels. The larger, 12¾ in. wide × 15½ in. high over black shading, features an oval garter and embellished the locomotives, which were black, lined red and yellow; it also appeared on the steam rail motors, of which there were once 19, and the composite motor trailer carriages.

The colours of the two designs were identical, but it will be noticed that there are differences in detail—in the riband carrying the motto and in the disposition of the year of incorporation. Both are dominated by the Welsh heraldic zoo . . . a jovial goat, a nanny in fact, and four lions whose air of sobriety is the very antithesis of the attitude struck by the dragon!

Taff Vale device for coaches

Brecon & Merthyr Tydfil Junction Railway

There were twenty-six subsidiary companies allotted to the Western group. Of the nine which owned locomotives and rolling stock, the Burry Port & Gwendreath Valley, the Cleobury Mortimer & Ditton Priors Light, the Llanelly & Mynydd Mawr and the Neath & Brecon eschewed any kind of heraldic *décor* externally. Of the others, reference had already been made elsewhere to the Welshpool & Llanfair Light, and the Brecon & Merthyr Tydfil Junction falls first to be dealt with alphabetically.

This company ranked fifth in size amongst the independent railways of South Wales and was incorporated in 1859. Its first section, from Brecon to Dowlais, was brought into use in 1863. In the same year the 'Old Rumney' Railway, from Rhymney Iron Works down the east side of the Rhymney valley through Maesycwmmer and Machen to Bassaleg was acquired. This was a former horse tramway, a decrepit concern, but with running powers over the Great Western into Newport it would put the Brecon & Merthyr on the road to the Bristol Channel when some very essential modernisation had been carried out. A branch to Merthyr (later made joint with the LNWR from Morlais junction) was opened in 1868 and in the same year the northern part of the system was linked with the southern by the completion throughout of a line between Dowlais and Pengam on the revitalised 'Old Rumney'. A 2¾ mile section of this link line, between Deri junction and Bargoed south junction, was owned by the Rhymney Railway, with which mutually satisfactory running powers were exchanged.

And with the Caerphilly branch, which had been opened in 1864, that was the Brecon & Merthyr . . . a hilly, sinuous north-south line, difficult to operate, slightly less than 60 route miles in length. It owned 47 locomotives, 115 coaching vehicles and 636 freight vehicles.

The company had two different heraldic transfers during its lifetime, which was rather odd, for it did not make a general practice of adorning either its brick red locomotives or its coaches of a browner shade with this sort of refinement. The earliest design, which is extremely rare, was based upon the seal. The full title, in gilt letters outlined in black, is displayed on a circular dark blue garter, edged in gilt and measuring 9 in. overall in diameter. Within this, on a curved red riband outlined in black, is carried the motto *Per ardua facile—Through difficulties easily* in gilt letters, again outlined in black. Beneath are shields depicting part of the seal of Brecknockshire (left) in gilt and black and part of the seal of Glamorgan County Council (right) in gilt, red and black. The latter was taken from the arms of the De Clare family, Lords of Glamorgan, which the County Council adopted and which were formerly assumed by Cardiff.

Whoever was responsible for this first armorial venture of the Brecon & Merthyr must have been allergic to the bats which appear on the Brecknockshire shield in the seal; he replaced them by bees, which have sometimes appeared in heraldry to denote industry. And he got away with it; there were bees again in the second and better known transfer!

This was a much larger design measuring 11⅛ in. wide × 13⅜ in. high, over black inner and brown outer shading in each case. It will be observed

:hat a conventional garter was introduced and the shorter and more :ustomary title was displayed. Within the garter the design was unchanged and in all respects the colouring was the same as that of its predecessor.

Brecon & Merthyr 1st device
W. H. D. Faulkner Collection

Midland & South Western Junction Railway

The MSWJ was a highly individual little north-south cross-country railway which ran from Andoversford junction, on the GWR Cheltenham–Oxford line, to Red Posts Junction at Andover, on the LSWR main line, thus linking Cheltenham and Southampton. It was created in 1884 by the merger of the Swindon, Marlborough & Andover and Swindon & Cheltenham Extension Railways, the first named having been opened between Swindon and Marlborough in 1881. Its headquarters were at Swindon and one of the most able railway general managers of all time, Sam Fay, rescued it from bankruptcy when he was in charge of the line from 1892 to 1899. At the end of 1922 its route mileage was nearly 61, excluding the Ludgershall–Tidworth branch, which was leased from the War Office. It then owned 29 locomotives, 134 coaching vehicles and 260 freight vehicles.

No coat of arms was adopted, but from 1914 onwards a distinctive gilt monogram 25 in. wide × 8 in. high made its appearance on the tender and tank sides of the locomotives, which were finished in crimson lake, as were the coaches, similar to the Midland shade. Only one example of the monogram is known to have survived and fortunately it is preserved in the British Railways Board Collection. It was designed by a member of the staff and is considerably easier to read than some of its Victorian predecessors.

As soon as the line became a subsidiary company of the Great Western, with which it had had many battles in the past, it was inevitable that its days would be numbered. During the last war it enjoyed an unprecedented temporary activity as a strategic route and soon after nationalisation it was divided between the Southern and Western Regions. Passenger train services ceased on 9th September 1961. Today all that remains of the MSWJ is a fragment at Swindon and the line from Andover to Ludgershall.

Midland & South Western Junction monogram
BRB Collection

Port Talbot Railway & Docks

This South Wales railway and dock undertaking was created specifically to tap a coalfield. It was incorporated in 1894 to acquire the existing harbour at Port Talbot, to construct a new dock there, and to build a railway thence through the Dyffryn valley coalfield to Maesteg in the Llynvi valley and on to the Great Western at Pont-y-rhyl junction in the Garw valley. Junctions in Port Talbot with the Great Western and the Rhondda & Swansea Bay Railways were also sanctioned.

The first section of line was opened on 1st September 1897 and the new dock in March of the following year. The Ogmore Valley extension, which took the Port Talbot to Pyle and Cefn, was opened in 1898 and the system was virtually completed when the working of the South Wales Mineral Railway, from Briton Ferry to Glyncorrwg, was taken over at the beginning of 1908. The route mileage owned or worked was 35 and 44 locomotives, a steam rail motor, 22 coaching vehicles and 411 freight vehicles made up the company's fleet.

A neat armorial transfer, introduced in 1897, was to be seen on locomotives and coaching stock. This has a diameter of 11 in. over dark brown shading and the deep emerald green garter is edged and ornamented in gilt, the lettering being gilt shaded black. Inside the garter there is a very natural looking Welsh lion, supported by a *chapeau*, which is a cap of maintenance or dignity; it is formed of red velvet (in this case generously edged in gold) and lined in ermine. Beneath is a formal red rose and the motto *Per Mare et terram—By sea and land*.

The smart 2-4-2 passenger tanks carried the transfer high up the cab sides, a practice some of the Irish lines followed.

Rhondda & Swansea Bay monogram for coaches
R. E. Vincent Collection

Rhondda & Swansea Bay Railway

The pleasantly named Rhondda & Swansea Bay Railway, like its neighbour the Port Talbot, was a subsidiary company of the Great Western. It, too, could boast an armorial transfer which was displayed on its neat black passenger and goods locomotives and chocolate coloured coaches. The latter also carried conventional monograms of the initials *RSBR*.

At the top of the design, in the place of honour, are the arms and supporters of the House of Jersey, together with the motto *Fidei coticula crux—The cross is the whetstone of (the) faith*; the seventh Earl of Jersey was the first chairman of the company. Beneath are depicted a sail-assisted

steam boat and an o-6-2 tank engine, the latter being quite a fair repesenta-
tion of one of the Kitson-built locomotives which hauled the goods and
mineral traffic of the line. At the base is the year of incorporation. All the
foregoing are placed on a dark green background, almost entirely surrounded, it will be seen, by the title of the company, the overall diameter
of the transfer being 9 in.

The first section of the Rhondda & Swansea Bay was opened from
Aberavon to the Rhondda Valley on 2nd July 1890, and the final section on
14th December 1894, when the little system extended from Treherbert
station on the Taff Vale Railway to Swansea, via Cymmer, Aberavon and
Briton Ferry. There were branches to Neath and Port Talbot docks,
making a total route mileage of 28¾.

A fleet of 27 locomotives, 90 coaching vehicles and 858 freight vehicles
was contributed to the Great Western.

Newport, Abergavenny & Hereford painted device
BRB Collection

Great Western Railway

That an armorial device can be thoroughly misleading as regards the
sphere of influence of the undertaking it represents is amply demonstrated
by the emblem of the Great Western, which was incorporated in 1835
for the construction of a railway between London and Bristol. Parts of the
achievements of these two cities were adopted as the company's insignia;

and there they remained until nationalisation in 1948, notwithstanding the extension of the system north to Birkenhead, west to Milford Haven, south to Weymouth and south-west to Penzance. It was as if the London & North Western had clung to the arms of the London & Birmingham throughout its life. But, of course, this didn't happen; Euston (Euston Square as it then was) coolly annexed Britannia and perhaps the shock of this arrogance was too much for Paddington!

During the growth of the Great Western several important railways were absorbed, of which the South Wales and the West Midland, taken over in 1863, the Bristol & Exeter in 1876, the South Devon and the West Cornwall in 1878, the Monmouthshire in 1880 and the Cornwall in 1889, are worthy of mention.

The West Midland was one of the keys to the future development of the company. It owned about 190 miles of line and leased or worked another 77 miles, having been created in 1860 by the merger of the Oxford, Worcester & Wolverhampton (dubbed *Old Worse & Worse*), the Newport, Abergavenny & Hereford and the Worcester & Hereford Railways. Of these, the second named possessed a coat of arms, a hand-painted example of which can be seen in the British Railways Board Collection. It is a replica of the company's seal and embodies the arms of Hereford (left) and Newport, Mon. (right). The Prince of Wales' feathers serve as a crest, as they did for more than one Welsh railway, especially on staff uniform buttons.

According to the authoritative *Livery Register of the Great Western*, published in 1967 by the Historical Model Railway Society, no trace can be found of any emblem in use on locomotives prior to 1887, when two singles, Nos. 9 and 55, were ornamented with a simple garter lettered *Great Western Railway*. Soon afterwards the first armorial transfer appeared on express locomotives, notably the class 3001 2-2-2s and the classes 439 and 717 rebuilt 2-4-0s. Available evidence indicates that in fact the transfer made its *début* on some of the clerestory roofed saloons.

This original transfer is illustrated. The shields of London (left) and Bristol (right) are given a massive backdrop of elaborate mantling and it will be noticed that the ship of Bristol is two-masted, with rather a Viking look about it, rides on natural water and is emerging from *behind* the castle. Neither the crests nor the mottoes of the two cities were embodied in the transfer, which measures $14\frac{3}{4}$ in. wide $\times$ $17\frac{3}{8}$ in. high over very heavy black shading. The colouring was generally akin to that of the final garter-cum-arms design in use during 1912–1922. The tenders usually carried a conventional Victorian monogram transfer of the initials *GWR*, a smaller version of which had ornamented some of the coaching stock before 1880.

Next to appear were three cast brass emblems, consisting of the crest of London, a divided shield representing London and Bristol within a garter, and the crest of Bristol, all of which are illustrated in order of display in unpainted form. When painted in the appropriate colours they made fine finishing touches on the single splashers of the elegant classes 3001 (rebuilt) and 3031 4-2-2s and on the leading splashers of the Badminton class 4-4-os. The two crests were not always worn; one engine at least, No 3021 *Wigmore Castle*, carried only the shield within a garter.

Great Western brass device for locomotives
Gerald Cattell Collection

In 1903 the second armorial transfer appeared. This is easily distinguishable from its predecessor because the shields denoting London and Bristol now had their appropriate mottoes *Domine dirige nos—O Lord direct us* and *Virtute et Industria—By virtue and industry* beneath them. Also the ship of Bristol had been Anglicised, was in full sail from a gateway of the castle and rode heraldic water. The castle was reputed once to have had an opening through which ships could pass to and from a protected area.

Transfers of the London and Bristol crests were made at the same time, but their display seems to have been restricted to main line coaching stock, on the sides of which they were fixed left and right respectively of the garter-cum-arms.

Differences between the 1903 and 1912 armorial transfers are trivial. The most noticeable are the slightly more circular outline and absent full point after *Company* of the second-named, which measures 14⅝ in. wide × 17¼ in. high over the customary heavy black shading; a smaller version of it, 5½ in. wide × 7 in. high, was produced for the adornment of Benn & Cronin train indicators at stations.

For the record it should be added that the author has traced at least one variant of each of the garter-cum-arms designs—pre-1903, 1903 and 1912— but the differences amount to nothing beyond a little more shading here and there in the garter or perhaps a minor change in the rigging of the ship or in the architecture of the castle in the shield of Bristol. They doubtless arose because transfers of all three designs were supplied by Butchers and Tearnes.

There was, however, another coat-of-arms transfer made by Tearnes during the period, of which neither date of issue nor purpose have been discovered. It is rather unusual in that it and the separate Bristol and London crests have a sepia finish and no other colour at all but for the gilt of the edging, ornamentation and lettering of the garter; in consequence, a curiously drab appearance has resulted. It was printed in three sizes, 12⅜ in. wide × 13¾ in. high, 13 in. wide × 13¼ in. high and 7½ in. wide × 10 in. high.

An uninspiring monogram also appeared. This was the prize-winning entry in a competition organised in the *GWR Magazine* in 1906 and it was to be seen on the steam rail motors, mercifully only for a few years.

By the end of 1922 the Great Western had become the longest British railway with a route mileage of 3,005. It owned 3,148 locomotives, 65 steam rail motors, 8,681 coaching vehicles and 80,693 freight vehicles.

The advent of grouping and the creation of a larger system by the addition of several lively Welsh railways afforded a glorious opportunity for the introduction of a new and more appropriate heraldic device, but it was not taken. Instead, the same old London and Bristol theme was trotted out in the company's fourth armorial transfer which began to appear on locomotives and coaches alike in 1928. But at least the garter and all the ostentatious mantling had disappeared and, at long last, London and Bristol were properly united with their crests as well as their mottoes. The transfer is 10⅜ in. wide × 12¼ in. high to the tip of the dragon's wing and it remained in general use up to nationalisation, except for a hiatus which had its beginnings in 1934 and lasted for about eight years.

A totem was the cause of the interruption. Eric Gill's notable efforts in helping to create for the LNER a recognisable house style had not

Great Western 3rd device

Great Western sepia device
W. H. D. Faulkner Collection

Great Western monogram for
steam rail motors

passed unnoticed at Paddington. And some enlightened official there was stung into action. A simple gold and black totem consisting of the company's initials in circular form was evolved, and whilst it may be said that there was nothing strikingly original about its design, it certainly made a neat emblem. The standard size transfer of it was given an overall diameter of 12 in., the gold letters having a width of $\frac{11}{16}$ in. with a black outline of $\frac{3}{32}$ in.

Sometimes referred to as a shirt button, it became the universal insignia of the Great Western, embellishing locomotives, carriages and containers, and uniforms, timetables and publicity material. But it was too much for certain diehard elements at Paddington and Swindon, whose parochial views prevailed in the end, and by 1942 the totem was on the way out. London and Bristol returned . . . which is where we came in!

Great Western circular emblem
Gerald Hartley Collection

Rhymney

Cardiff

Brecon & Merthyr final device

Taff Vale (locomotives)

PLATE 11

Port Talbot Railway & Docks

Rhondda & Swansea Bay

Great Western 1st device
W. H. D. Faulkner Collection

Great Western final device

PLATE 12

PART FOUR

Southern Railway and Predecessors

London & South Western Railway

One of our oldest companies, the London & South Western, came into
existence as long ago as 25th July 1834, when it was incorporated as the
London & Southampton. To woo the inhabitants of Portsmouth, however,
the name was changed by an Act of 4th June 1839, and so after a life of
less than five years it is hardly surprising that original examples of the
hand-painted London & Southampton device are extremely rare. The
design was even more simple than that of its contemporary, the London &
Birmingham, in common with which it adopted the dragon's wing of
London as a crest. Within a garter London (left) was represented also by
its familiar cross and sword of red on a white background and (right)
Southampton by its arms of 1575, consisting of two red roses on white
above a white rose on red, representing Lancaster and York.

The London & South Western retained the dragon's wing as a crest in
its own device, in which the shield within the garter was divided into
five parts instead of the customary quarterings. In the left half are denoted
London and Southampton. In the opposite half are representations of
Salisbury, consisting simply of eight bars alternately gold and blue;
Winchester, five silver castles and two gold lions on a red ground, a
reminder of the days when the town was the capital of England; and
Portsmouth, a six-pointed *estoile* above a crescent moon, both gold, on a
blue ground, which was the badge Richard Coeur de Lion, creator of the
naval base there, adopted on his crusade.

Beautifully cast plaques of this design, hand-painted, adorned each
side of the Beyer Peacock class 46 4-4-0Ts and class 380 4-4-0s of 1879,
centrally above the numbers on tank and cab sides respectively. The
transfer produced later embellished certain classes of locomotives and
coaches; it measures 9¾ in. wide × 16¾ in. high and is shown on the

125

locomotive sage green in use during the company's last years. Old recor
of Tearnes indicate that there was a smaller version $7\frac{3}{4}$ in. wide $\times$ $13\frac{1}{4}$ i
high which was available either with a blue garter or a red garter.

London & Southampton painted device
BRB Collection

Concurrently with the armorial transfer the London & South Wester
employed a variant which differed in two quite important respects. A
ancient 2-2-2 locomotive took the place of the dragon's wing as a cres
and the shield was quartered by dropping Salisbury. This design appeare
in rust red on the company's headed stationery for a time, and in fou
colours on the front cover of the timetables.

A staff uniform button is also reproduced. This, it will be observed
embodies a quartered shield, again without Salisbury, and is devoid of
crest.

The London & South Western was the largest constituent company o

London & South Western monogram on 4-4-0 No 563
BRB Collection

London & South Western gilt uniform button (23mm dia)
David Swan Collection

See
Supplement
p. 10

the Southern, to which it contributed a well managed system of 1,02
route miles and 912 locomotives, 3,818 coaching vehicles (including 18
electric motor cars and 148 electric trailer cars) and 14,625 freigh
vehicles. The electric stock was always given an exterior finish of sag
green, lined-out in orange chrome and black, but its adoption for th
steam-hauled coaching vehicles, which wore an attractive livery of umbe
brown with light golden brown (often described as 'salmon') uppe
panels, did not take place until 1918.

London, Brighton & South Coast Railway

The Brighton, as it was popularly known, was the smallest of the three
constituents of the Southern. Nevertheless, it contributed 619 locomotive
and a rail motor, 2,591 coaching vehicles (including 50 electric moto
cars and 84 electric trailer cars) and 10,151 freight vehicles. And with
only 457 route miles of line it carried more originating first class pas
sengers than either the North Western or the Great Western.

It was formed on 27th June 1846 by the amalgamation of the London &
Croydon and London & Brighton Railways, which had been incorporated
in 1835 and 1837 respectively. It is believed that the former of these never
displayed an heraldic device, but the London & Brighton gave itself a
most opulent-looking coat of arms which must have set the fashion for
subsequent LB & SC heraldic exercises. The Royal crown was flaunted
as a crest, resting upon a *motif* of roses, thistles and what would appear to
be shamrock. Beneath were two rather ornate shields denoting London
and Brighton (two dolphins) above the full title of the railway.

London & Brighton uniform buttons, which had a silver finish, embodied
the same components, but arranged in a manner identical with that of the
company's seal.

After the formation of the London, Brighton & South Coast an even
more elaborate coat of arms made its appearance. A locomotive head-on
now formed the crest and fearsome-looking dragons from the City of
London arms acted as supporters. Of the four shields between the latter
London was rightly denoted in the upper one, then clockwise followed

London & Brighton painted device
Museum of Science & Engineering Newcastle-upon-Tyne

London & Brighton silver finish uniform button (23mm dia)
David Swan Collection

London, Brighton & South Coast painted 1st device
Museum of Science & Engineering, Newcastle-upon-Tyne

London, Brighton & South Coast gilt uniform button
(23mm dia)
David Swan Collection

the Cinque Ports (three demi-lions conjoined to three demi-ships), Brighton and Portsmouth (six-pointed *estoile* and crescent moon).

An unexpected and unusual feature is the appendage at the base of the design, in which the legend LOCO & CARRG SUPERINTENDENT surrounds a monogram of the initials JCC. This would have been J. C. Craven, who had assumed that office in 1847, and the coat of arms was undoubtedly displayed on his inspection coach.

A specimen of the earliest LB & SC uniform button is reproduced. Like its L & B predecessor, it was a replica of the seal.

Two magnificent cast iron examples of the first LB & SC device, much simplified and paired with the arms of Edward Alleyn, have been preserved in the British Railways Board Collection and one is illustrated. Born in 1566, Alleyn was a successful actor-manager associated with Shakespeare. When he retired a wealthy man in 1604 he bought the Manor of Dulwich and built upon it almshouses, a school and a chapel. The school flourished and in 1882 was divided, one part as Dulwich College and the other as Alleyn's School. The Peckham-Sutton line of the LB & SC, completed in 1868, traversed the property between Tulse Hill and East Dulwich. The cast iron panels bearing the two shields were fixed to the parapets of bridges on this section, and delightful splashes of *décor* they must have made.

The next device to come on the scene was the first transfer of the company's arms and this is unlikely to have been later than 1881; it may well have been much earlier. It will be seen that there is a close resemblance to the first design, but there are three important differences. The locomotive crest has been supplanted by the less original dragon's wing of London; the title has had *Railway* added; and, of course, there is no appendage. The transfer measures 18 in. wide × 13½ in. high and, until the close of the century, seems to have been confined chiefly to special vehicles such as saloons. The coach livery in those days was varnished mahogany, picked out with gilt lines, and the vehicle numbers were sometimes displayed within a blue garter carrying the company's name in gilt serif letters.

Brighton was made a county borough in 1897, when six martlets, birds akin to swallows and, in heraldic practice, usually shown without legs, were added to its coat of arms as a form of border.

This change led to the early introduction of a new transfer, 20 in. wide × 18 in. high, which was the third LB & SC armorial device. Although still ornate, it was more compact than its predecessor. The crest was now displayed above the ornamentation, which had been tidied up. A more orthodox kind of shield was quartered with the arms of the four leading places on the system and, incidentally, rearranged to corres-

pond with the four points of the LB & SC compass–London, Brighton
Hastings and Portsmouth. And the title was displayed in unbroken form
The arms of Hastings differed from that of the Cinque Ports, which had
been displaced, only in that a complete lion appeared between two demi
lions/demi-ships instead of there being three of the latter; this centre
lion is believed to have been introduced into the arms of Hastings when
the town was made head of the confederation. The other change concerned
Portsmouth; an eight-pointed *estoile* had taken the place of the previous
six-pointed specimen.

LB&SC device and Edward Alleyn's arms on bridge panel
BRB Collection

The third design was to be seen on special vehicles such as the luxuriou
five-car Royal train of 1897, Royal Mail vans, the two family saloons o
1903, the Directors' saloon of 1913 and, experimentally, on 4-4-0
locomotive No 60. The two family saloons of 1903 introduced a new
livery of umber brown with white upper panels, but this style was com
paratively short-lived, for in 1910 all-over umber brown, lined black and
edged yellow, was adopted and remained until the end of the company's
existence.

Umber brown, lined black and edged in gold or yellow, had been
assumed as the passenger locomotive livery in 1905, displacing the
extravagantly tricked-out golden ochre. A monogram of the initials
LB & SCR in *serif* letters made its first appearance at the same time on the
then new Atlantic express engines. Its use was extended to many of the
other passenger tender engines, but after a few years a *sans serif* monogram
replaced it.

Another 4-4-0 locomotive, No 73, was experimentally decorated
about 1905 with hand-painted versions of the quartered shield in an oval
garter on her leading splashers, after the adoption of the umber brown

livery. They were displaced later by transfers not, as one would expect, of the current coat of arms design, but of its predecessor of 1881 or *ante*, probably because stocks of the latter were still on hand and its depth made it more suitable for locomotive splasher display. Other passenger tender engines, such as 4-4-0 No 59 and some companion B4 class engines, Atlantics Nos 39, 41 and 424, and the Brighton Works 0-6-0 shunting tank, were eventually similarly embellished. Because of the hallow depth of their splashers, the ornamentation above and flanking the dragon's wing crest was omitted from the transfers worn by the Atlantics.

Thus North Eastern and North Western practice of exhibiting armorial transfers of two different designs concurrently on locomotives and coaches was emulated for a period by the Brighton, albeit to a much limited extent.

London, Brighton & South Coast 4th device
BRB Collection

If the locomotives were somewhat deficient in an armorial sense this was not the case where the stationery was concerned. Much LB & SC notepaper was embossed or printed with the coat of arms at the head, and three quite different types have been traced, plain embossed, blue and full colours.

The final transfer of the company's arms, and the fourth design since 1846, was produced in about 1908. It consisted simply of a shield, devoid of crest and supporters, quartered similarly to the preceding design (save that Portsmouth had a newer moon) and surrounded by a blue garter carrying the title in gold *sans serif* lettering. Its purpose has not been satisfactorily established, for it was never displayed on locomotives or rolling stock so far as the author is aware. Yet, paradoxically, it is probably the best known of all the LB & SC designs for it appeared in full colour in W. J. Gordon's *Our Home Railways* which, first published in 1910, was one of the 'bibles' of contemporary young railway enthusiasts.

South Eastern & Chatham Railway

The device of this railway reflects the duality of its constitution, which was adopted under an Act of 1st August 1899. The arms of the South Eastern and of the London, Chatham & Dover, side by side, are encircled by a band bearing the legend *South Eastern and Chatham Railway Companies Managing Committee*. The transfer has a diameter of $15\frac{3}{4}$ in. over black shading, and decorated the Brunswick green locomotives and reddish brown coaching stock; its display on the locomotives ceased when a livery of dark grey was assumed during the 1914–18 war.

Although they were worked as a unified system the two companies were not amalgamated. They appeared separately with their Boards of Directors in *Bradshaw's Railway Manual, Shareholders' Guide & Directory* until its final issue of 1922, together with the Managing Committee. The latter was presided over by Cosmo Bonsor, the South Eastern Chairman and included six other directors from each company. Under the agreement blessed by Parliament, net receipts were split 59 per cent to the South Eastern and 41 per cent to the London, Chatham & Dover, and new capital was raised in the same proportions.

The South Eastern was the senior of the two railways, having been incorporated on 21st June 1836. It also embraced two of the oldest railways in the south of England, the Canterbury & Whitstable, opened in 1830, and the London & Greenwich, opened in 1836 and notable as London's first railway. Its original main line, from Redhill, on the London & Brighton, to Dover via Tonbridge, Ashford and Folkestone, was completed in four instalments, being brought into use throughout on 7th February 1844. From Redhill South Eastern trains initially reached London Bridge over the metals of the London & Brighton, London & Croydon and London & Greenwich Railways. London Bridge became the headquarters of the line.

Dover Castle formed part of the seal and the arms of Dover embellished some of the early first class carriages. The appellations *Dover Railway* or

London & Dover Railway sometimes appeared in the earliest official publications. And when a transfer of the company's arms was eventually produced for the decoration of locomotives and carriages, Dover Castle was embodied as the crest, with the white horse of Kent superimposed centrally. The shield contains a demi-lion conjoined to a demi-ship to represent the Cinque Ports, all of which the South Eastern served, beneath which there is a red cross to denote London, with the sword of St Paul omitted, bearing at its centre another white horse of Kent. At the base is the motto *Onward*, which dates back to the seal.

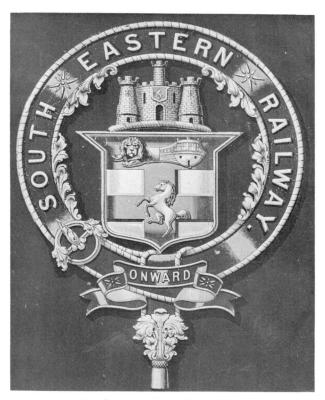

South Eastern device for coaches

There are two versions of this transfer, one having a buff garter shaded grey and the other an Oxford blue garter shaded light blue. The first was for display on James Stirling's medium green passenger locomotives and the other was worn by the dark lake carriages. In all other respects the two versions were exactly alike and measure $9\frac{3}{8}$ in. wide $\times$ $12\frac{5}{8}$ in high over black shading. Of the blue gartered version there was also smaller replica 7 in. wide $\times$ 10 in. high.

The full achievement was to be seen on gilt uniform buttons, one of which is illustrated, and on the covers of the public timetables. The supporters fitted in extremely well. On the left is a sea-lion from the arms of Kent, appropriate for a railway with maritime interests, and on the right is a London dragon somewhat more jovial looking than those on the LB & SC arms.

South Eastern gilt uniform button (20mm dia)
David Swan Collection

On 4th August 1853 the East Kent Railway was incorporated to build line from the South Eastern at Strood to Canterbury. Two years later powers were obtained to push southeastwards from Canterbury to Dover and the route throughout was finally completed from Strood to Dover on 1st November 1861, having been opened in stages. By this time the next extension, westwards from Strood to St Mary Cray, with London as the goal, was well in hand. On 1st August 1859 the company changed its name to *London, Chatham & Dover* and its first trains to enter Victoria station of the LB & SC, pending completion of its own half of that station did so on 1st December 1860. Victoria became the headquarters.

Whereas the South Eastern ran through much of Kent, penetrated Sussex and Surrey and flung out a long arm to Reading, the LC & D was content to serve the Garden of England. The white horse of Kent, descended from the white horse on the standard of the chieftain Horsa, who headed the first Saxon settlement in the Isle of Thanet, therefore made an appropriate crest, with *Invicta* as a motto. Both were to be seen on gilt uniform buttons and on the company's armorial transfer with which the varnished teak coaching stock was emblazoned. A gilt monogram sufficed for the black express locomotives which, however, were relieved by grey lining edged vermilion on the outer side and yellow on the inner.

The first device, which was hand-painted, is believed to have displayed within a garter four shields bearing the white horse of Kent and the arms of Rochester, Canterbury and Faversham. Chatham, curiously, was omitted, possibly because its neighbour Rochester was a cathedral city and considerably older. In the transfer, which measures $12\frac{1}{4}$ in. wide $\times$ $12\frac{1}{2}$ in. high over shading, the white horse of Kent takes pride of place. The arms of Rochester are beneath it (note the gilt old English 'r' in the centre of the cross), London is on the left and a representation of Dover is on the right. The latter is derived not from the Borough's seal but from the seal of Robert de Hathbrand, onetime Abbot of St Martin's Priory, Dover. His seal of 1345 had a black field with a cross and four leopards' heads in silver; these rather sombre colours were replaced by red and gold respectively in the transfer.

Some LC & D stationery was headed with a simple and very elegant arrangement of the device in red outline. Perhaps the noblest examples were in cast iron, the best known being those once contained in the fabric of the bridge straddling Ludgate Hill, within the shadow of St Paul's. This bridge carries the line to Holborn Viaduct and not far away, at the south end of Blackfriars bridge, is a less familiar example, which is illustrated. Surmounting the arms is a large V under a Royal crown and an English rose; it bears the year in Victoria's reign in which the line was opened, 1864.

It is more than likely that the South Eastern and London, Chatham & Dover would have come together of their own volition very much earlier than they did but for the advent of Sir Edward Watkin on the Board of the former in 1864. He became Chairman in 1866 and between him and James Staats Forbes, his opposite number on the LC & D, there developed a feud which lasted nearly thirty years and became a byword. Suffice it here to say that the senseless competition and duplication of facilities which ensued in the rivalry between the two last English 'Railway Kings' impoverished their companies. Within five years of Watkin's resignation in 1894, through ill-health, the working union had become reality.

London, Chatham & Dover cast iron device on Blackfriars
bridge
Photo: Michael Andress

London, Chatham & Dover gilt uniform button (25mm dia)
David Swan Collection

138

The South Eastern & Chatham ended up with 729 locomotives, 8 steam
l motors, 3,691 coaching vehicles, 11,345 freight vehicles and a public
age which was a legacy of some embarrassment to the Southern in its
mative years.

London, Chatham & Dover monogram

Railways in the Isle of Wight

here were fourteen subsidiary companies in the make-up of the Southern
ilway. Only four of them, the Isle of Wight, the Isle of Wight Central,
e Freshwater, Yarmouth & Newport and the Plymouth, Devonport &
uth Western Junction, owned any locomotives and rolling stock. None
uld boast a coat of arms.

Tearnes did, however, produce garter transfers for the Isle of Wight
d Isle of Wight Central, in all cases for the display of coach numbers,
d three of them are illustrated because of their rarity.

The oldest design is the first highly ornamental garter of the Isle of
Vight Railway, dating back before 1885. Two main colours are employed,
edium blue for the body of the garter and gilt for the remainder, the
rnamentation being shaded dark brown and the lettering dark blue. The
rter has a diameter of 9¾ in. over shading and the title is pock-marked
ith unnecessary full points. A larger variant 9¼ in. wide × 10 in. high,
ithout any ornamentation, was printed in 1885.

Finally there is the more orthodox garter of 1915, in this case shown
ith a coach number. It measures 10¼ in. wide × 13 in. high over black
ading the garter being Brunswick green and the numeral gilt with red
ading and white highlights, the rest being gilt. There is a variant of this
ansfer, which differed only as regards the body colour of the garter,
hich is Oxford blue.

The Isle of Wight Railway was incorporated in 1860 and ran from
yde St Johns Road to Ventnor, with a branch from Brading to Bembridge,

Final Isle of Wight garter

Early Isle of Wight garter
W. H. D. Faulkner Collection

Isle of Wight Central garter

London & South Western
(locos and coaches)

London & South Western (publications)
BRB Collection

n, Brighton & South Coast 2nd device

London, Brighton & South Coast 3rd device

PLATE 13

South Eastern (locomotives)
W. H. D. Faulkner Collection

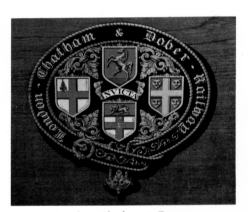

London, Chatham & Dover

South Eastern & Chatham

Southern painted coat of arms

PLATE 14

initial section from Ryde to Shanklin being opened in 1864. It had a
ute mileage of 15¼ and was the most prosperous of the three railways
the island.

First to be authorised and opened was the Cowes & Newport, brought
to use on 16th June 1862 and operated jointly with the Ryde & Newport
hen the latter was opened in 1875. Twelve years later the merger of these
o lines with the Isle of Wight (Newport Junction) Railway which, in
e arms of a Receiver, tried to make an honest living out of the Sandown–
erstone–Newport line, produced the Isle of Wight Central. From
erstone the Newport, Godshill & St Lawrence Railway built southwards
Ventnor and in 1913 was absorbed by the Central, by which it was
orked, bringing that company's route mileage up to 28½.

The garter transfer worn by the teak coaches of the Isle of Wight
entral measures 12¾ in. wide × 14¾ in. high over shading, which is
ack throughout. The body of the garter is vermilion and all else is gilt.
ere was a smaller version 9½ in. wide × 11½ in. high and both were
inted in 1893. With the bald legend *Central Railway* the design has an
prepossessing air about it, a characteristic also of the railway of which
was the insignia.

Southern Railway

or the greater part of its life the Southern did not possess a coat of arms.
hen modernising its stations, at which it was very good, some heraldic
xcursions were occasionally indulged in, but these were in the form of
surrecting the devices of its predecessors. The booking hall of the
constructed Ramsgate station was such an example. An expedient was
be seen in the company's board room, where there was a circular
s-relief device quartering the arms of London, Dover, Brighton and
outhampton in the full heraldic colours. It is now preserved in the
ritish Railways Board Collection.

The most noticeable feature of the Southern was its use of green. Its
xpress passenger locomotives, its passenger stock, its timetable covers . . .
l were green. At its stations, with their green and cream woodwork,
een vitreous enamel plate, lettered white, was universally employed
r all signs, including those on signal boxes, and they did much to unify
e undertaking. Eventually, a distinctive form of legend *SOUTHERN
RAILWAY* was evolved in what might best be described as 'sunshine'
ttering. It became a familiar feature on renovated station fascias and
sewhere.

In 1938 the Southern emulated the Great Central and the London North Eastern by seeking full armorial bearings from the College of Arm. Unfortunately the war intervened and the Letters Patent, signed an sealed by the three Kings of Arms, were not finally dated until 6th Marc 1946.

The achievement adopted is of particular interest because it reflecte to some extent contemporary heraldic design and, at the same time demonstrated how markedly it differed from that of the Victorian era. This is best exemplified by the multiple crest: the double disc wheel the latest steam locomotives of the company; the flash through it to denot the extensive electrification; the wings above to indicate the speed both forms of traction; and the sun as a backdrop, a subtle reminder of th onetime Southern slogan *South for Sunshine*.

Acting as supporters are the red dragon of London and the white hors of Kent, each using a double disc wheel as a hind foot rest. The shield h a field of heraldic water to represent the coastal areas served. The sma shields upon it, adorned with a sword, a leopard's head, a dolphin and rose, of course denote London, Dover, Brighton and Southampto respectively.

What a pity that the Southern, like the LNER before it, made n transfer of its device! Instead, its public display was limited to tw vitreous enamel plates, one fixed each side of the *Battle of Britain* Pacifi No 34090, which in 1949 was named *Sir Eustace Missenden* after th company's last General Manager who became the first Chairman of th BTC Railway Executive. The shield, however, did appear on one or tw prestige publications, of which the Ashford works centenary booklet wa one.

The example illustrated is a faithful full size replica of the actual devic copied by the vitreous enamellers, handpainted at York carriage an wagon works for the author in 1949. It measures 17 in. wide × 18 in. high

In I have seen both Severn lots of the central mantlepiece —

The St George cross is shown with a very thin white areas disagreements

surrounding

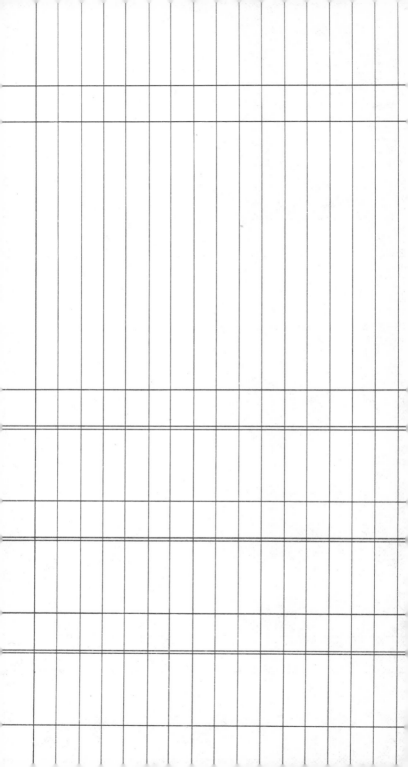

PART FIVE

London Transport and Predecessors

Central London Railway

Because of its uniform fare of twopence for any distance with which it was opened, the Central London Railway was immediately nicknamed the 'Twopenny Tube'. Incorporated in 1891, its first section, from Shepherds Bush to the Bank, was brought into public use on 30th July 1900. By the time the existence of the company came to an end in 1933 its line had been extended eastwards to Liverpool Street in 1912, westwards to Wood Lane in 1908 and thence, over the Great Western, to Ealing Broadway in 1920.

Neither the electric locomotives with which it began operations (and which were replaced by motor coaches because of property owners' complaints of vibration) nor the two standby steam locomotives were embellished heraldically in any way. But motor coaches and trailers, which were finished in a brown and cream livery closely akin to that of the Great Western, were decorated with a neat device centrally beneath the waist line of each car, just below and between the words *Central* and *London*. Like the Maryport & Carlisle coat of arms, it bore neither name nor motto, and was unique in that two of its quarters represented parishes. Before the formation of the metropolitan boroughs in 1899 the vestries of the London parishes were the effective local government bodies in the metropolitan districts.

In the first quarter is denoted the City of London, in the second the parish of St George, Hanover Square (St George and the dragon), in the third the parish of St Marylebone (the Virgin and Child between two lilies taken from the arms of Barking Abbey), and in the fourth the county of Middlesex. The dragon's wing from the City of London's arms acts as a crest and surmounts the shield. Overall the transfer measures $7\frac{1}{2}$ in. wide $\times$ $12\frac{1}{8}$ in. high. It has become something of a rarity since it went out of use in about 1925.

City & South London device
Photo: London Transport

City & South London Railway

See supplement
p. 10

The City & South London was seven years earlier on the scene than th
Central London, having been incorporated in 1884 as the City of Londor
& Southwark Subway. It was, in fact, the pioneer tube railway in the world

In 1890 the name of the company was changed to *City & South Londo*
and later in the same year, on 18th December, the first section fron
King William Street to Stockwell, was opened to the public. Eventuall,
the line extended to Clapham Common in the south and to Euston, vi
Moorgate and Angel, in the north.

No armorial device appears to have been generally employed during th
company's independent existence, save on uniform buttons. Both locomo
tives and coaches were devoid of any external ornamentation, but th
emblem illustrated has survived. For what purpose it was produced is no
known. The two shields denote London (left) and the Southwark cross
commemorating the martyrdom of St George (right); the latter wa
originally the mark of the Bridge House estates of the City of London and
appeared in the third quarter of Southwark's coat of arms, granted in 1902
But apart from these there is little heraldic about the design. In the upper
portion is depicted London Bridge, crowned by triple lamp-posts and

146

carrying pedestrians, a horse bus and a hansom cab. In the river in the foreground are two steamboats and a rowing boat with four seagulls thrown in for good measure. And beneath the river are two tunnels containing the leading and trailing ends of electric trains.

The uniform button design presented a much less crowded effect consisting, it will be seen, of a *quatrefoil* within the surrounding title, inside which are contained shields carrying the arms of London and the Southwark cross, with what at first sight looks like a cockatrice as a crest, but is much more likely to be a wyvern with (unlike that of the Midland) forelegs. The cockatrice had no associations with the City of London whereas the earliest form of the City's supporters in its device was a wyvern. Alternatively the designer may have confused the wyvern with the dragon, which supports the City's arms nowadays and which it closely resembles.

Excluding the Waterloo & City Railway, which was built in close association with the London & South Western and absorbed by it in 1907, there were three other tubes which ultimately became part of London Transport. They began as the Baker Street & Waterloo, the Charing Cross, Euston & Hampstead, and the Great Northern, Piccadilly & Brompton and were united in 1910 to form the London Electric Railway. Today they are integral parts of the Bakerloo, Northern and Piccadilly lines and neither they nor the London Electric adopted any distinctive emblem.

City & South London nickel uniform button (27mm dia)
David Swan Collection

Metropolitan District Railway

The nucleus of London Transport was the Metropolitan District Railway which was incorporated in 1864 and was generally known as the District Railway to distinguish it more readily from the company of which it was originally an offshoot, the Metropolitan. Fate decreed that the two rail ways should be bitter opponents for many years, for in the early 1870s the District came under the control of James Staats Forbes of the London Chatham & Dover, and the Metropolitan under that of his rival, Sir Edward Watkin of the South Eastern.

On Christmas Eve 1868 the first section was opened from South Kensington to Westminster. By 1900 District tracks had been extended westwards to Ealing Broadway, Hounslow and South Harrow, although the latter section had not been opened. Wimbledon and Richmond were reached partly over the LSWR. In the east the Inner Circle had been forged by a joint link with the Metropolitan and another, jointly under construction with the London Tilbury & Southend, was to put the District on the road to Barking.

Electrification was carried out during 1903–1905, beginning with the South Harrow line, under American auspices. In 1900 Charles Tyson Yerkes, representing a wealthy United States syndicate, had bought the

Metropolitan District in stained glass
Photo: London Transport

powers of the Charing Cross, Euston & Hampstead tube, and a year later, effective control of the District. The strong American look of the red District cars, whether they had clerestory roofs with domed ends, or elliptical roofs of similar end outline, was to last for many years to come.

In the first two decades of electrification the maroon cantrails of most of the cars were lettered *District Railway*, the words being spread the length of the vehicle between the end doors in American fashion. A small proportion of motor coaches and trailers, similar to those of the District, and interchangeable with them, were likewise lettered *LTS Railway*. These were for working part of the services to and from Barking over the White-chapel & Bow Railway and were owned by the London, Tilbury & Southend.

Heraldry was unlikely to flourish under such circumstances, but in its steam days the District often employed an armorial device on its maps and timetables. The example illustrated is from a painted glass window in

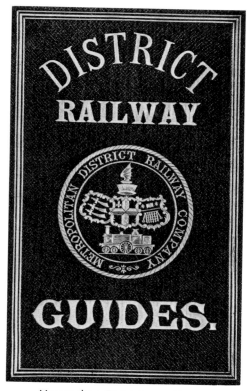

Metropolitan District on guide cover
Photo: London Transport

149

the company's board room at Electric Railway House, Westminster. Beneath a helmet bearing the dragon's wing crest from the City of London arms are three shields representing Middlesex (left), City of London (centre) and City of Westminster (right). At the base is a 2-2-2 Bury style locomotive with a haystack firebox and cylinders arranged *à la Rocket*, quite unlike any steam locomotive ever running on the District or anywhere else!

A similar design in gold graced the head of some of the company's stationery. The locomotive was now a 2-2-2T with a decent cab and inside cylinders and looked as though it really *was* capable of doing a job of work. The version which appeared in gilt on the black leather covers of the District Railway Guides is worthy of illustration. It will be seen that in this case the heraldic stationer concerned obviously had a prediliction for J. Pearson's double bogie broad gauge monstrosities of the one-time Bristol & Exeter Railway!

Metropolitan Railway

To a city solicitor, Charles Pearson, must go much of the credit for bringing to reality the first underground railway in the world, which was opened between Bishop's Road and Farringdon Street in London on 10th January 1863. Due to his enthusiasm and energy the necessary capital was raised for what in those days was a prodigious enterprise which, it was claimed, would fully solve London's traffic problem!

The company formed to carry out the building of the line was incorporated as the North Metropolitan Railway in 1853 and, a year later, re-incorporated as the Metropolitan Railway. A junction was to be effected with the Great Western at Bishop's Road and, doubtless because the Great Western had put up £185,000 of the capital and was to work the line, it was laid to a mixed gauge, namely the customary 4 ft. 8½ in. and Brunel's nonconformist nonsense of 7 ft. 0¼ in. This unsatisfactory situation was rectified by the removal of the broad gauge rails six years after the opening of the line.

By the end of the century the Met. was linked to the District at South Kensington and had completed the Inner Circle with that company by a joint line from Aldgate to Mansion House; another connected at Shadwell with the East London (of which the Met. was one of five lessees) whose metals ran to New Cross. Westwards, by means of lines jointly owned with the Great Western, it reached Hammersmith and Uxbridge Road.

But it was in the north-west that the development of the Met. had been most striking. From Baker Street a main line now extended to Aylesbury, with a branch to Chesham; from Aylesbury the line continued to Quainton Road, whence a branch line tapped Verney Junction and the Wotton Tramway, which had been leased, ran to Brill; and at Quainton Road also the London extension of the Great Central joined the Met.

So far the company had relied entirely upon steam traction, which was featured in its first armorial transfer. A hexagonal shield, which was bordered with the company's title in gilt letters, shaded red, on a Cambridge blue background, contained the arms of London, with the motto *We work for all* in gilt on the red cross. Beneath were two tunnel portals in a brick wall, with a steam locomotive leaving the left hand one and the tail end of a passenger train framed within the other. The shield was surrounded by much gilt ornamentation, the overall dimensions being 19 in. wide × 13 in. high.

Metropolitan 1st device as a cast iron gate plaque
Photo: London Transport

A similar but simplified version was to be seen in the form of a circular cast iron plaque on an iron gate at Harrow-on-the-Hill station.

In both designs the trains were shown wrongly as keeping to the right. No doubt the error arose because of somebody's confusion over heraldic terminology; the *dexter*, or right, and the *sinister* or left sides of a shield are as seen by the bearer of the shield, not by the beholder. The slip-up was rectified in the second design of transfer produced soon afterwards, which was in all other respects identical with the first, and is illustrated. Most unusually the transfer was displayed on the sandbox sides above the leading splashers of the smart deep crimson lake 0-4-4T and 0-6-2T engines and, inappropriately, on the earliest electric rolling stock.

In 1904 the Harrow–Uxbridge line was opened and in the following year this line, the main line to Baker Street and the Inner Circle were electrified. Shortly afterwards a new coat of arms transfer was produced and this embellished steam and electric locomotives and passenger rolling stock for some years.

Metropolitan device in Board Room chair
BRB Collection

The new design was affluent with crimson and ermine mantling, which served as a back drop to a shield quartered with the enlarged realm of the Metropolitan, namely London (top left), Middlesex (top right), Buckinghamshire (bottom left) and Hertfordshire (bottom right). A clenched fist radiating electrical energy formed the crest and beneath was the motto *Vis vincta servit*—*Strength subdued serves*. So far as the author is aware this design represents the only example of the swan of Buckinghamshire (family badge adopted by the youngest son of Edward III, Thomas of Lancaster, who was created Earl of Buckingham with the crowning of Richard II in 1377) on a railway heraldic device. The hart of Hertfordshire was, of course, also to be seen on the Great Eastern emblem. Overall, the final Metropolitan coat of arms transfer measures 16 in. wide × 14 in. high.

Expansion of the Met. continued until the end of its independent existence. After the transfer of its lines northwards from Harrow to a joint undertaking known as the Metropolitan & Great Central Joint Committee in 1906, it took over the Great Northern & City electric line from Finsbury Park to Moorgate in 1913, electrified the Met. & GC line as far as Rickmansworth in 1925 and completed a new branch to Watford (owned jointly with the LNER) in the same year. For the last-named, single-deck buses, emblazoned with the Met. coat of arms, ran between Watford station and the High Street. The company's last new line, from Wembley Park to Stanmore, was opened in 1932 and in the following year the Met. lost its separate identity within the embrace of the newly constituted London Passenger Transport Board.

The Met. did not employ a universal symbol, but from 1915 onwards its station name signs consisted of white letters on an Oxford blue bar across a solid red diamond, akin to the bull's eye station name signs of the District Railway and the tube lines; a green diamond was used on the East London Railway. The diamond and bar emblem of the Met. perhaps lost a little of its impact because it was identical in shape and colour with the contemporary trade mark of a well advertised disinfectant rejoicing in the name of Milton!

Metropolitan gilt uniform button (24mm dia)
David Swan Collection

London Transport

The beginnings of London Transport may be said to date back to the year 1902, when the Underground Electric Railways Company of London Ltd was registered to carry out the electrification of the District Railway. This was followed by the construction and equipment of the three tubes which in 1910 merged to form the London Electric Railway and in 1912 a scheme for fusion with the London General Omnibus Company was completed. The Central London and City & South London Railways came under the control of the Underground Electric Railways Company in 1913.

By this time the famous bull's eye sign had made its *début*, but not in quite the same form as it is today. It was first employed as a name sign at stations on the District Railway and on some of the tube lines in 1909, when the station name, in white letters on an Oxford blue background, was displayed across the face of a large red disc. In the previous year it had been agreed to use the word *UndergrounD* on illuminated horizontal or vertical signs at station entrances; a solid disc was placed behind the horizontal forms of this symbol from 1913 onwards. In that year the London General Omnibus Company dropped its trademark of a spoked wheel with crossbar and wings and began to use a bar carrying the legend *General* across a circle.

In 1916 Frank Pick, then Commercial Manager, commissioned Edward Johnston, a distinguished lettering artist, to design and cut a new type fount for the improvement of Underground signs and notices. The *sans serif* type Johnston evolved is still in use today and its beauty and clarity is equalled only by the lettering created by his pupil, Eric Gill. It was at this time that Johnston carried out a design exercise for the Underground, one consequence of which was the emergence, in 1917, of the now familiar bar and circle symbol. This distinctive device was soon to be seen at stations, at bus and tram stops and on printed publicity. Eventually it appeared on railway rolling stock, trolley buses, Green Line coaches and in many other places.

No other transport undertaking, before or since, has equalled the thoroughness with which the standard lettering and symbol were brought into use. That both have survived is due to their simplicity and excellent proportions, and the bar and circle device loses nothing of its superb recognition value when it is used, as it often is, without any lettering at all. Needless to say, it has its imitators in this country and other parts of the world.

On 13th April 1933 the London Passenger Transport Board was incorporated to take over and merge the railway undertakings of the

Central London, City & South London, London Electric, Metropolitan
and Metropolitan District, the tramways in the London area and practically
all the bus and coach companies there too, headed by the London General
Omnibus Company, the operative date being 1st July.

Original bull's eye station name sign
Photo: London Transport

Modern bar and circle station name sign
Photo: London Transport

155

Early silver button on bus driver's uniform
Photo: London Transport

Present day black uniform button
Photo: London Transport

As subsequent events proved, the decision made then to adopt the shorter title *London Transport* as a fleet name and for general purposes was a wise one. With nationalisation in 1948 the statutory title was changed to *London Transport Executive*, responsible to the British Transport Commission. Then in 1963, with the dissolution of the latter, it became *London Transport Board*, responsible to the Minister of Transport. And since the beginning of 1969 it reverted to *London Transport Executive*, responsible to the Greater London Council. Through all these questionable changes in the corridors of power the bar and circle emblem was left unruffled and serene.

When the statutory title *London Transport Executive* was first assumed a Temple Bar griffin was adopted as the seal. This, too, has survived and may be seen today on staff uniforms, embroidered in the cloth and embossed on the buttons. It also makes a pleasant heraldic touch on prestige publicity material from time to time.

Embroidered griffin on present day uniform
Photo: London Transport

157

Central London

Metropolitan 2nd device

Metropolitan final device

PLATE 15

Cheshire Lines Committee final device

Donegal
BRB Collection

County Donegal Joint Committee

PLATE 16

PART SIX

Jointly Owned Railways and Rolling Stock and Rolling Stock Companies

Carlisle Citadel Station Committee

In all but the early issues of the nostalgia-evoking Junctions Diagrams book, published by the erstwhile Railway Clearing House, it was Carlisle and not Clapham (as the layman might expect) which took pride of place on page 1. In the halcyon days before 1923 the Citadel station there was a paradise for the visiting railway enthusiast, who was regaled with the locomotives and rolling stock of four English and three Scottish companies . . . Caledonian and London & North Western, Midland and Glasgow & South Western, and North British, North Eastern and the little Maryport & Carlisle.

Carlisle Citadel nickel uniform button (23mm dia)
David Swan Collection

For such a multitude some kind of common administration was clearly essential and in 1873 the Carlisle Citadel Station Committee, on which all were represented except the Maryport & Carlisle, was set up to control the station and its approaches either side, which were Caledonian and London & North Western joint property. The staff uniforms were adorned with distinctive nickel buttons embellished with the arms of Carlisle, one of which is reproduced.

A similar organisation, known as the Goods Traffic Committee (Caledonian, Midland, Glasgow & South Western and LNWR) was established to control goods lines west of Citadel station and there was yet a third body, the Dentonholme Joint Committee (Midland, Glasgow & South Western and North British), under whose *aegis* came Dentonholme goods depot and its approach lines.

All three joint bodies were assigned to and disappeared within the LMS.

Cheshire Lines Committee

When the Cheshire Lines Committee lost its identity in British Railways it was the largest jointly owned railway in the country, with 143 miles of line, 267 coaching vehicles and 44 goods brakes. At one time it possessed its own freight vehicles, but the motive power for domestic needs was always met by the Manchester, Sheffield & Lincolnshire and its successors the Great Central and the LNER. When it passed to the ownership of the LMS and LNER in 1923 it operated no less than 4,573 freight vehicles and a road fleet of 92 goods and parcels motors and vans.

The Cheshire Lines was created in 1865 by the fusion into one concern of the Cheshire Midland, the Stockport & Woodley Junction, the Stockport, Timperley & Altrincham Junction and the Garston & Liverpool, all of which were owned jointly by the Manchester, Sheffield & Lincolnshire and the Great Northern Railways. The West Cheshire and the Liverpool Central Station & Railway were added and the arrangement was legalised by the Cheshire Lines Transfer Act of 5th July 1865. The Midland Railway came in as a third partner in 1866 and in the following year the Cheshire Lines was given full independence of status as a separate undertaking with a common seal by an Act passed on 15th August.

In common with other railways, Cheshire Lines coaching stock always of varnished oak brown in external finish, passed through a four wheeled infancy to a six-wheeled childhood. Its early maturity with bogie vehicles, magnificent twelve-wheelers, began in the 1880s. With their appearance it is believed that the first transfer of the Cheshire Lines armorial device was to be seen, two emblazoned on each side of the body beneath a monogram of the letters *CLC* centrally above on the waist.

Cheshire Lines Committee 1st device

Cheshire Lines Committee 2nd device without decorative
surround
W. H. D. Faulkner Collection

The transfer measures $20\frac{3}{4}$ in. wide $\times$ $15\frac{3}{4}$ in. high over black inner
and brown outer shading and its components, and their arrangement,
follow the design of the seal. At the top, a shield embraces a rose and
thistle *motif* above three lions *passant reguardant* (left) and a lion *rampant*

163

(right) to denote the Great Northern; below (left) is the arms of the Manchester, Sheffield & Lincolnshire (as illustrated in Plate 6); and alongside (right) are those of the Midland (as illustrated in Plate 4).

After the Manchester, Sheffield & Lincolnshire changed its name to Great Central in 1897, and had received a grant of arms in the following year, a new Cheshire Lines transfer was produced. This embodied the Great Central coat of arms in place of the MS & L device, but there was no other alteration in design, colour or size.

Each of the Cheshire Lines transfers had a variant devoid of all the ornamentation outside the garter, which measures 11¼ in. wide × 13 in. high. One of them is reproduced.

County Donegal Railways Joint Committee

Owned equally by the Great Northern of Ireland and the Midland of England, the County Donegal Railways could rightly claim to be not only the longest narrow gauge system in the British Isles but also the second longest of those joint lines which had both locomotives and rolling stock, being surpassed only by the Midland & Great Northern Joint Railway. Its engines worked 125 route miles of 3 ft. gauge line.

The parent company was the Finn Valley Railway, incorporated in 1860 to build a standard 5 ft. 3 in. gauge line between Stranorlar and Strabane. It was opened in 1863 and worked by the Irish North Western (later Great Northern). Its headquarters were at Stranorlar station and over the entrance to its offices there was displayed its armorial device, which was a replica of its seal.

A chevron, with two owls above it and one beneath, occupy the shield; the crest is a coronet; the supporters are a vulture (left) and a griffin (right); and the motto is *Be just and fear not*. The design is derived from the achievement of the Hewitt family, of whom Viscount Lifford was Chairman of the company. Later he held a similar position on the West Donegal.

In 1879 the West Donegal Railway was incorporated for the construction of a 3 ft. gauge line from the Finn Valley station at Stranorlar to Donegal. The first section, as far as Druminin, was opened in 1882. By this time the Finn Valley, which now had rolling stock of its own (but was still worked by the Irish North Western) and a financial interest in the West Donegal, agreed to work the line. Donegal was finally reached in 1889 and three years later the Finn Valley and West Donegal were amalgamated to form the Donegal Railway.

The seal of the West Donegal was adopted both as the seal and as the coat of arms of the new company. It consisted simply of the arms of the

Conyngham family, who owned much of the land traversed between Stranorlar and Donegal, side by side with that of Londonderry, above the legend *Tyrconnel*. The transfer for application to the green locomotives and chocolate coloured coaches was made by Tearnes in 1898 and has a diameter of 9⅛ in.

Conversion of the Finn Valley tracks to 3 ft. gauge was completed in mid-July 1894. In the previous year the Donegal–Killybegs line was opened and in 1895 traffic began on the Stranorlar–Glenties line. The system was completed with the opening of the Strabane–Londonderry and Donegal–Ballyshannon lines in 1900 and 1905 respectively.

Finn Valley in stone at Stranorlar
Photo: P. Sunderland

Purchase of the Donegal Railway by the Great Northern and th
Midland was legalised on 1st May 1906. In consequence, the Strabane
Londonderry line was transferred to the Midland, but the newly forme
County Donegal Railways Joint Committee continued to operate it. Th
Strabane & Letterkenny Railway, opened in 1909, was also worked by th
County Donegal.

The new armorial transfer was circular, of the same diameter as it
predecessor and a fair reproduction of the seal. This time the arms of th
O'Donnell family, the Lords of Tyrconnel, formed the basis of the design

Black, lined red, became the locomotive livery in 1906. It was change
to geranium red and black lined white in 1937. For various periods th
coaches were successively black and cream, plum and cream and blac
all over. The latter funereal garb was changed to red with cream uppe
panels to blend with the final livery of the locomotives.

After the last war a continuous decline in traffic receipts set in. Th
Glenties branch was closed in 1947 and services on the Strabane–London
derry line ceased at the end of 1954. The last day of 1959 saw the cessatio
of all regular rail services on the remainder of the system.

East Coast Joint Stock

The East Coast Route to Scotland, from London (Kings Cross) to Edinburgh
(Waverley), Glasgow (Queen Street) and Aberdeen via the Forth and Ta
bridges, was created by the natural alliance of the Great Northern, Nortl
Eastern and North British Railways, which were destined to form th
backbone of the LNER.

Haulage of the Anglo-Scottish trains was the responsibility of the Grea
Northern from London to York, of the North Eastern thence to Edinburgh
and the North British onwards, and vice versa. In 1860 the Great Northeri
suggested that a jointly owned stock of carriages should be provided for
the through services. The idea was adopted and by the following year
fleet of 50 had been formed; by 1873 it had grown to 89.

The vehicles were finished externally in the varnished teak of the Grea
Northern and over the years joint ownership was indicated by *ECJS* ir
monogram or in *serif* lettering, or by the legend *East Coast*. It was not long
however, before armorial transfers made their appearance, the first desigr
of which resembled that of the Great Northern final device. A thistle anc
a rose formed the crest and the shield was quartered by the three lions o
England, the lion of Scotland, Edinburgh and London.

It was unusual to see London relegated to the fourth quarter. The same
arrangement was followed in the design of the gilt buttons of the trair

East Coast Joint Stock 1st device

East Coast Joint Stock monogram

On East Coast Dining Car Express
between ENGLAND & SCOTLAND

190

East Coast Joint Stock device in colour on stationery

167

Scottish arms for 1st class ECJS coaches

English arms for 1st class ECJS coaches

staff uniforms and in the coloured heading to the stationery one could obtain on the trains. In both cases the use of the description *East Coast Railways* will be noted.

By the early 1890s a new armorial transfer appeared. This measures 11¾ in. wide × 14 in. high over brown (outer) and black (inner) shading. It is a much tidier effort than its predecessor because the representations of the two countries and two capitals, still in the same order, are contained within a garter. The colours are almost entirely confined to gilt, white, red and pink.

This transfer was usually applied, below the waistline, to the central panels of 3rd class coaches (the East Coast companies abolished 2nd class on all their main lines on 1st May 1893). But on the sides of the 1st class vehicles, including dining and sleeping cars, an heraldic extravaganza was inaugurated before the turn of the century. The ECJS emblem, again displayed centrally, was flanked by the arms of England at one end and those of Scotland at the other, left and right respectively! The transfers of these national devices are chiefly tinted gilt, red, buff and pale greyish green, and they are enormous. The English emblem measures 21¾ in. wide × 26 in. high, the Scottish a half inch wider and a quarter inch higher.

What an impressive effect one recalls they gave on their rich varnished teak background, with its red and gold beadings!

East Coast Joint Stock gilt uniform button (23mm dia)
David Swan Collection

Furness and London & North Western joint lines

In bygone days there was quite a large complex of half-a-dozen differe railways in the area of West Cumberland lying between Maryport a Cleator. And of the three small fry, the Cleator & Workington Junctio the Rowrah & Kelton Fell and the Whitehaven, Cleator & Egremont, t last-named was the longest and the most 'compleat' as regards locomotive rolling stock, stations and workshops of its own. It was also the only o of the trio to boast any kind of emblem.

The Whitehaven, Cleator & Egremont was created by the presence iron ore, like the Furness, with which it was connected in the south. was incorporated in 1854 and its first sections, from Mirehouse junctio just outside Whitehaven, to Egremont and to Frizington, were open for goods traffic in the following year. Eventually it extended from Sell field in the south to Marron in the north, embracing a total route mileag of 35.

When the company was jointly acquired by the Furness and the Lond & North Western Railways under an Act of 1878 its seventeen immaculate maintained green locomotives, lined out red and white, were transferre to the Furness. The coaches wore a chocolate livery and the device whic adorned their sides is reproduced.

Today it is something of a rarity. The simple design portrays on fo shields the activities of the area served by the line. In the chief position depicted a rather toy-like 2-2-2 well tank locomotive of a type th company never possessed. A three-masted sailing ship (a WC & E lin reached the Irish Sea at Parton), sheaves of corn and an ironworks mak up the rest.

The design measures $11\frac{3}{4}$ in. wide $\times$ $10\frac{1}{4}$ in. high overall and ver unusually, was made up as a transparency and not as a transfer.

Great Western and London & North Western joint lines

With their territories contiguous or interlaced at many places, it is n surprising that there once existed several stretches of railway owne jointly by the Great Western and the London & North Western, th longest being the Shrewsbury & Hereford, $82\frac{3}{4}$ miles including branche All of them were operated by locomotives and rolling stock of the paren companies and none indulged in any kind of emblem.

One of the progenitors of the second longest, however, the $56\frac{1}{2}$ mile system of the Birkenhead Joint Committee, did possess a coat of arms, hand-painted specimen of which is preserved in the British Railways Board Collection. This was the Birkenhead, Lancashire & Cheshire Junction Railway, which was incorporated in 1847 and amalgamated in the same year with the Chester & Birkenhead.

Birkenhead, Lancashire & Cheshire Junction painted device
BRB Collection

In the first quarter of the ornamental shield a lion represents Birkenhead, the abbot's crozier in the centre being taken from the ancient arms of Birkenhead Priory; the present day coat of arms of Birkenhead, granted in 1878, embraces emblems to represent Tranmere, Bebington and Oxton as well. In the second quarter the feudal Lords of Manchester are denoted. And the third and fourth are occupied by the unusual divided device of the city and county of Chester, which was also to be seen in the arms of the Grand Junction Railway.

The name of the company was changed to *Birkenhead Railway* in 1859 and as from the beginning of the following year it was leased to the Great Western and London & North Western, which took possession on 18th November.

Hammersmith & City Railway

From the Metropolitan at Bishop's Road, the western end of the world's first underground railway, the Hammersmith & City, a Great Western venture incorporated in 1861, built a line to Hammersmith, with a branch to Addison Road, which was reached over West London tracks from a point near Uxbridge Road. Both were opened in 1864, when relations between the Great Western and the Metropolitan happened to be at their worst, and the Met. evinced no interest in the line. But after *rapprochement* had taken place the H & C was vested jointly in the two companies in 1867. By the time it was electrified towards the close of 1906 it had become an integral part of the Met. network.

Hammersmith & City emblem

After electrification two services were operated with H & C stock, which was entirely of the open type made up into 3-car sets, namely Hammersmith–New Cross (East London Railway) and Edgware Road–Addison Road (West London Railway).

Some H & C stock was owned by the Great Western (the farthest it ever got in the way of electrification) and some by the Met., which was responsible for all the servicing and maintenance. The cars were completely Met. in appearance and were finished in that company's varnished teak style. But closer inspection revealed the fact that the legend *Metropolitan Great Western* was emblazoned the length of the cantrail on one side and, so as to cause no hard feelings, *Great Western Metropolitan* on the other.

The dual ownership was also indicated on the H & C monogram below the waist where, once again, the courtesies of precedence were exchanged on a strict basis of equality. There is not much to be said about the design. The gilt *H & C* is displayed on a pale sea green background, the surrounding ornamentation being tinted pale green and buff. The riband carrying the

itle is pink, buff edged, the lettering being black, shaded red. The
ransfer measures 17¾ in. wide × 13¾ in. high over black shading.

Altogether it is the least attractive of all the colourful railway devices
f its time.

North Union painted device
BRB Collection

ancashire & Yorkshire and London & North Western joint lines

1 1830 the Wigan Branch Railway was incorporated with powers to
uild a line to Wigan from the pioneer Liverpool & Manchester Railway
t Parkside junction. In the following year the Wigan & Preston Railway
vas authorised. The two companies were complementary and when they
nerged as the North Union on 22nd May 1834 the occasion was note-
vorthy in that it afforded the first example of railway amalgamation to be
anctioned by Parliament.

The North Union adopted the arms of Preston as its insignia and a hand-
ainted specimen preserved in the British Railways Board Collection is
eproduced. The letters *PP* are said to stand for *Proud Preston*, according to
ome of its neighbours.

In 1844 the Bolton & Preston, incorporated in 1837, which joined at
uxton junction, was absorbed and the North Union took the form of an
nverted Y. But its days of independence were numbered. From the

beginning of 1846 it was leased jointly to the Grand Junction and Manchester & Leeds, being vested in these companies on 27th July 1846, less than a fortnight after the Grand Junction had itself become part of the London & North Western. The Manchester & Leeds changed its name to Lancashire & Yorkshire in the following year. Much later still, in 1889, the former North Union line from Parkside junction to Euxton junction was vested in the LNWR and the Bolton to Euxton junction section became part of the L & Y. Only the stem of the Y, from Euxton junction to Preston, including Preston station, remained joint property.

Lancashire & Yorkshire and London & North Western
parcels van device

See Supplement
p. 11

The largest joint enterprise of the two big companies was the Preston & Wyre Railway, which had been incorporated in 1835. It was taken over fourteen years later, being vested two-thirds in the L & Y and one-third in the LNWR, and eventually developed into a little network of 46 miles serving the area lying between Preston, Lytham, Blackpool and Fleetwood.

Although it possessed no emblem, some of the cartage vehicles were armorially embellished. The parcels vans, which were painted black, carried on each side a 10 in. wide × 6½ in. high transfer which combined the arms of the L & Y and LNWR in full colour. One of them is illustrated the other was the same, save that the names of the owning railways were reversed! There were smaller versions 6 in. wide × 4¾ in. high.

Manchester South Junction & Altrincham Railway

One of our oldest joint railways was the Manchester South Junction & Altrincham, which was promoted as an independent company in 1844

Its backers were the Manchester & Birmingham, the Sheffield, Ashton-under-Lyne & Manchester, and Lord Francis Egerton, Earl of Ellesmere. The noble lord's involvement was short lived, however, for his interest was bought in 1847 by the two railways mentioned, by which time they had become part of the newly formed London & North Western and Manchester, Sheffield & Lincolnshire companies respectively.

The MSJ & A consisted of a main line 'dog' of only 1¾ miles from Store Street (later London Road, now Piccadilly) station to the former Liverpool & Manchester Railway near Ordsall Lane, wagged by a branch line 'tail' of 7¾ miles from Castlefield junction, near Knott Mill, to Altrincham. The first section, from Oxford Road to Altrincham, was opened on 20th July 1849.

A daily service of 26 trains (13 each way) was instituted in which the passengers were conveyed in coaches owned by the MSJ & A; motive power was provided by the Manchester, Sheffield & Lincolnshire, as in the case of the neighbouring Cheshire Lines. By the turn of the century the line was annually coping with 146 passenger trains daily and booking 5 million passengers at its 9 stations.

If the coat of arms which was emblazoned on the sides of the varnished mahogany coaches struck some as ornate, it did at least portray the beginnings of the line. In the centre is part of the arms of Lord Francis Egerton; Manchester, originally the headquarters of both owning railways, is denoted above and their projected terminals, Birmingham and Sheffield,

Manchester South Junction & Altrincham in carpet

are represented left and right; the position at the base is occupied by Altrincham. The transfer measures 16¾ in. wide × 16½ in. high over black (inner) and dark brown (outer) shading.

The device was repeated, in full colours, in the very rich looking carpets with which the first class compartments were once equipped, a section being reproduced.

When the MSJ & A was converted to electric traction in 1931 by its then owners, the LMS and LNER, the 24 new three-car sets were given a distinctive external livery of Brunswick green, lined black and yellow. They were emblazoned with the armorial transfer right up to the nationalisation of the railways in 1948. *See supplement p. 11*

Midland & Great Northern Joint Railway

Only fragments of this once important cross-country system now remain. At its zenith it possessed 183 route miles of line, excluding its share of the Norfolk & Suffolk Joint Committee, which was owned jointly with the Great Eastern. It extended from an end-on junction with the Midland at Little Bytham, and from the Midland and the Great Northern at Peterborough, in the west, to Cromer, Great Yarmouth and Norwich in the east. For domestic services it was entirely self-contained with some 98 locomotives, 225 passenger vehicles, 388 freight vehicles and a cartage fleet of its own.

The system was made up of a variety of small railways, the oldest of which was the Norwich & Spalding, opened from Spalding to Holbeach in 1958 and thence to Sutton Bridge four years later. This and other companies west of Kings Lynn eventually came together to form the Midland & Eastern. An Act passed in 1877 ratified the merger and also the arrangement by which the Midland and the Great Northern provided the train services and the administration. The connecting Peterborough, Wisbech & Sutton Bridge was worked by the Midland.

East of Kings Lynn development was similarly in the hands of small companies . . . Lynn & Fakenham, Yarmouth & North Norfolk and Yarmouth Union. These were amalgamated on 1st January 1883 to form the Eastern & Midlands Railway and six months later the Midland & Eastern and Peterborough, Wisbech & Sutton Bridge were brought into the fold. On 9th June 1893 the Midland & Great Northern Joint Committee was incorporated and the Eastern & Midlands was vested in it as from 1st July of the same year.

Of all these companies only the last named provided itself with an armorial transfer for its locomotives and passenger stock. It was a very

East Coast Joint Stock final device

Whitehaven, Cleator & Egremont

Manchester South Junction & Altrincham

PLATE 17

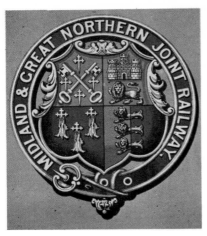

Pullman Car Company 1st device

Midland & Great Northern Joint final
device

West Coast Joint Stock

Somerset & Dorset Joint final device

PLATE 18

Eastern & Midlands device
BRB Collection

Midland & Great Northern 1st device
W. H. D. Faulkner Collection

Midland & Great Northern 2nd device
W. H. D. Faulkner Collection

neat device with the name of the railway in black *sans serif* letters on a white garter which encircled a shield quartered by the arms of the See of Peterborough, Norwich, Kings Lynn and Great Yarmouth. They are denoted respectively by the two crossed keys between four *cross crosslets fitchée* (with the base arm pointed); the castle and lion; the three erect dragons' heads, with the jaws of each pierced with a *cross crosslet fitchée*; and the three demi-lions *passant reguardant* conjoined to the bodies of as many herrings.

This design was adopted by the Joint Committee in 1893 when the rather unusual title *Joint Midland & Great Northern Railway* was embodied in black *sans serif* letters on the white garter. This did not last for long and a variation with the more usual *Midland & Great Northern Joint Railway* next appeared. There were no colour changes.

At the beginning of 1910 the final design of M & GN armorial device made its appearance. Once again the only alterations were in the garter. This was now Oxford blue, which made a much more attractive foil than white to the gilt edging of the garter and the shield, and the colouring of the lettering was changed from black to gilt to match. The transfer measures 9¾ in. wide × 10¾ in. high over black shading.

In 1935 the LMS and LNER, as successors to the Midland and Great Northern, agreed that the local administration of the line should be assumed by the LNER and this took effect on 1st October 1936. To all outward appearances the M & GN now began to lose its aura of individuality. But the name remained proudly until the end, which came on 28th February 1959, when the main closure of the system took place to save British Railways an estimated £1 million a year.

Pullman Car Co Ltd

The original British Pullman Car Company was set up in 1882 and all cars running in Great Britain were built in the United States until the appearance of those introduced on *The Southern Belle*. This was the first all-supplement Pullman express, which was put on between London and Brighton in 1908, at a time when the interests of the company had been acquired by the late Lord (then Mr) Dalziel. The cars on that train and all subsequent cars were constructed in this country.

In 1915 the Pullman Car Company Ltd was formed to take over the Dalziel cars, stock, work in hand and goodwill of the original concern. There were then 77 cars and arrangements were in force for their operation on the London, Brighton & South Coast, the South Eastern & Chatham, the Metropolitan and the Caledonian. They wore an umber brown and cream livery, except for those on the South Eastern & Chatham, which were finished in crimson lake. This latter colour was adopted for the cars assigned to the Metropolitan in later years and for those introduced on the Great Eastern.

The Pullman armorial device, which consisted of parts of the arms of the four countries of the British Isles, formed a prominent feature of their décor. Externally, all cars had one transfer $15\frac{3}{4}$ in. wide × $14\frac{1}{4}$ in. high applied at each end on each side, below the waist line. Internally, on a $9\frac{1}{2}$ in. diameter plaque above each end door, a smaller transfer of the arms, $6\frac{5}{8}$ in. wide × 6 in. high was usually displayed, together with the car name (if 1st class) or number (if 3rd class).

Pullman metal device for uniforms

Pullman in formica table top

After the grouping of the railways in this country and in Eire, Pullman cars began to range much farther afield. They continued to serve the Brighton and South Eastern sections of the Southern, but a new client, the London & North Eastern, now operated them into the West Riding and to Scotland. In Ireland, cars were run on services from Dublin to Cork, to Limerick and to Sligo during the years 1925 to 1936. In the latter year the Great Southern took them over; they were not the success in Eire they had been elsewhere.

In 1946 neat metal replicas of the Pullman coat of arms, enamelled in full colours and measuring $1\frac{7}{16}$ in. wide × $1\frac{3}{8}$ in. high, were introduced as lapel badges for the staff in the cars.

A year or so later buff formica table tops made their appearance, and these were imprinted with a modernised version of the Pullman arms in five colours. A specimen is reproduced. The shield is red, lined in black, and the use of red and brown in the first and second quarters has the effect of making the lions of England and lion of Scotland difficult to distinguish. The brown Irish harp stands out better on a pale blue background and the red Welsh dragon is prominent enough on white. The supporters are brown, their features picked out in black, and the ornamentation is also brown. The title is shown in white letters, shaded black, on a red riband having a black reverse side. The overall measurements are $6\frac{5}{8}$ in. wide × $5\frac{5}{8}$ in. high.

The British Transport Commission bought all the Ordinary share capital of the company as from the beginning of July 1954, when the fleet totalled some 206 cars. And in 1959 a new coat of arms design produced by Tearnes heralded the developments which were to make 1960 a peak year in Pullman history.

Three sizes of transfers were made, following basically the same design. The smallest measured 19 in. wide × $8\frac{1}{2}$ in. high and was put into general use on the existing units, which were now universally painted the umber brown and cream livery. It was also allotted to 44 new cars under construction by Metropolitan–Cammell Carriage & Wagon Company for East Coast Route services. In practice, however, it was found that the new transfer did not stand out sufficiently, and so a second version was prepared, $22\frac{3}{8}$ in. wide × 10 in. high, not only larger but with the colours in the shield a little brighter.

This has since remained the standard design for umber and cream cars and is reproduced. Apart from the components of the shield and the title, the finish is a bronze colour with plentiful highlights, as in the case of its predecessor. The lions of England are bronze on a red field, the Scottish lion red on yellow, the Irish harp bronze on light Royal blue and the Welsh dragon red on white. The legend *PULLMAN* is in yellow *serif* lettering shaded brown, on a red background. Altogether it is a very striking design.

The third version is larger still and measures 36 in. wide × 16 in. high. It was produced for the embellishment of the beautiful blue Pullman diesel expresses which made their bow in 1960 on the London Midland and Western Regions. The transfers were not only applied to the coach sides but to the ends of the motor coaches at each end of the train. Their colour is the same as the two smaller designs, save that the Irish harp has a pale brown background.

On 1st January 1963 the Pullman Car Company became a wholly owned subsidiary of the British Railways Board. There is little doubt that the name will live on for many years to come to connote luxury in rail travel.

Pullman present day device, 2nd version

Somerset & Dorset Joint Railway

Few railways can have inspired such affection as the Somerset & Dorset. No doubt the loveliness of the country it traversed, the amalgam of its main line and branch line workings over a sinuous, stiffly graded road, much of it single track, and the individuality of its locomotives, rolling stock and stations, had much to do with it.

It began by a merger of the Somerset Central and the Dorset Central in 1862, and when its line from Evercreech to the Midland at Bath was opened in 1874 the little system took the form of a Y, with its arms from Burnham and Bath meeting at Evercreech and its stem running thence to Wimborne. There was, in addition, a line from Glastonbury to Wells. The Midland and the London & South Western jointly leased the Somerset

183

& Dorset in 1876 and, over the years, transformed it into a model cross-country line which won the loyalty of the staff who served it. The through traffic stimulated between Bath and Bournemouth called for a cut-off line, from Corfe Mullen to Broadstone, which was opened in 1885. Five years later the branch from Edington Junction to Bridgwater was completed, making the total route mileage 105½.

A view of a train passing Glastonbury Abbey and Glastonbury Tor and, on the right, the arms of Dorchester, formed the seal of the Somerset & Dorset. When it became a joint line a coat of arms was devised which featured the arms of Bath on the left and those of Dorchester on the right. In the design of Bath the wall with the heraldic water above denotes the Roman baths and the sword, with the key superimposed, the Abbey church of St Peter and St Paul. The Dorchester design is based upon a 14th century seal comprised of a castle with three towers bearing the Royal arms as used from 1340 to 1405. Curious features are that Bath includes, as it should, a key, which is missing from the design of the City arms, whilst Dorchester shows 'modern' France, with three *fleurs-de-lis*, whereas the Borough Council's design depicts 'ancient' France, with an indefinite number of *fleurs-de-lis*.

The transfer produced measured 9 in. wide × 12 in. high and it differed from the plate only in the colour of its garter, which was green. It did not last long and was supplanted by the blue gartered version illustrated, which is identical in all other respects.

Passenger locomotives and coaches, which were given an external finish of Prussian blue, lined out black and yellow, were emblazoned with the transfer. The striking livery was retained until 1930 when the line, which had been vested jointly in the LMS and Southern on 1st July 1923, underwent fundamental changes by which its responsibilities were shared out between its owners. After nationalisation more changes followed, ending up with the Western Region in control of the line in 1958. This must have been the last straw for the staff, who had never had any love for the Great Western and who, before the end, publicly demonstrated their complete lack of confidence in the Western Region management.

The last trains ran on 6th March 1966, leaving open only a fragment or so for freight traffic, as in the case of the M & GN. A journey by coach from Bath to Bournemouth now takes over 3½ hours; the train needed little more than a couple.

West Coast Joint Stock

A fleet of coaches owned jointly by the London & North Western and Caledonian Railways for their West Coast Route services between

England and Scotland was created in the middle 1860s. This was the period when the Caledonian successively absorbed the Scottish Central and the Scottish North Eastern, so giving the West Coast partners metals of their own beyond Glasgow to Edinburgh, Perth and Aberdeen.

West Coast Joint Stock was finished in the LNWR coach livery of purple lake below the waist and spilt milk above. Tearnes produced an appropriate emblem measuring 10¾ in. wide × 10¼ in. high over black shading for transferring to the purple lake. The red shield, which bears a gilt Scottish lion, has gilt ornamentation. Beneath is a red rose and thistle *motif* largely consisting of lime green leaves. Then follows some more gilt ornamentation and finally the legend *West Coast Joint Stock* in black letters on a red background.

Altogether it is an extremely neat and now somewhat rare transfer. There were no other heraldic excursions, such as those in which the competing East Coast partners indulged!

PART SEVEN

Great Southern Railways
and Predecessors

Cork & Macroom Direct Railway

Because of its good dividend record the Cork & Macroom Direct was described as 'one of the plums' when the time came for it to be absorbed by the Great Southern in 1925. The line was incorporated in 1861 and built to the standard Irish gauge of 5 ft. 3 in. between the places in its title, starting from Capwell terminus in Cork. It was brought into public use on 12th May 1866 and when the Great Southern take-over occurred it was being operated with 5 locomotives, 30 coaching vehicles and 101 goods vehicles. The route mileage was 24½.

Cork & Macroom Direct painted device
BRB Collection

Cork & Macroom Direct nickel
uniform button
(17mm dia)
David Swan Collection

The company's arms, which were simply those of Cork, are preserved in the British Railways Board Collection, but it is not known to what use they were put because it was not the practice to display them on the locomotives and coaching stock. The nickel buttons to be seen on staff uniforms were ornamented with a shield bearing the Cork arms, with an ancient locomotive beneath. A specimen is reproduced.

Regular passenger services on the Cork & Macroom Direct ceased on 29th June 1935. Freight and cattle services were continued for some years, on an increasingly infrequent basis, and the last trains ran on 10th November 1953 for the monthly fair at Macroom.

Cork & Muskerry Light Railway

The northern neighbour of the line to Macroom was the 3 ft. gauge Cork & Muskerry Light Railway, known variously as the *Blarney Tram* or the *Muskerry Tram*; the farming district north west of Cork consists of the baronies of Muskerry. It, too, enjoyed some financial success before going into oblivion.

Cork & Muskerry key plate for garter
W. H. D. Faulkner Collection

Cork & Muskerry nickel uniform
button (25mm dia)
David Swan Collection

Incorporated in 1883, the first section of 8½ miles, from Western Road terminus in Cork to Blarney, was built in six months and opened to the public in August 1887. The line from Coachford Junction to Coachford was brought into use in 1888. The branch from St Ann's to Donoughmore, built by a separate company and worked by the Cork & Muskerry, was opened in 1893, making the total route mileage of the little system 26½. Some 7 locomotives, 27 coaching vehicles and 53 goods vehicles were needed for its operation.

The company possessed no armorial device, so far as is known. But in 1887 Tearnes put in hand a garter emblem, presumably for the coaching stock, and the black and white key plate of this is reproduced. The nickel uniform buttons, which had an unusually large diameter of almost an inch, were embossed with the arms of Cork.

Under Great Southern auspices the line continued to function until the losses sustained through bus and lorry competition could no longer be ignored. The last day of operation for all traffic was 29th December 1934.

Cork, Bandon & South Coast Railway

The oldest and largest of the four railways centred upon Cork was the Cork, Bandon & South Coast, which was incorporated in 1845 as the Cork & Bandon and opened between those places six years later. The remainder of the system was mostly built by separate companies eventually absorbed by the Cork & Bandon, which adopted the wider title in 1888. The main line finally extended from Cork to Baltimore, a distance of 61¾ miles, with branches to Kinsale, Clonakilty and Bantry; running powers were exercised over the Timoleague & Courtmacsherry Light Railway from

Cork & Bandon nickel uniform button (19mm dia)
David Swan Collection

Supplement
P 11

Ballinascarthy Junction on the Clonakilty branch to Courtmacsherry. Altogether the CB & SC owned 65¾ miles of line and worked another 28¼.

A Cork & Bandon uniform button of nickel finish, a great rarity, is illustrated. Its design was adopted for the armorial transfer brought into use after the title *Cork, Bandon & South Coast* was assumed and applied to locomotives and coaching stock alike, all of which were given a livery of sage green with black bands edged yellow on each side.

The transfer measures 8 in. wide × 8¾ in. high. Within the garter are the year of incorporation and a shield quartered by the arms of Cork and an adaptation of the seal of Bandon. The latter embodies a seven-arched bridge with a domed and embattled gateway at each end and an escutcheon surmounted by an earl's coronet in the centre. In the transfer it will be seen that this is changed to a five-arched bridge with three simple beflagged towers.

When the company became part of the Great Southern its contribution included 20 locomotives, all of them tanks, 68 coaching vehicles and 445 freight vehicles. The entire system was closed by Coras Iompair Eireann on 1st April 1961.

Cork, Blackrock & Passage Railway

The Cork, Blackrock & Passage adopted the arms of Cork as its device, which contained a splendid example of the sailing ship between the two towers, and was emulated in this way by the younger Cork & Macroom and Cork & Muskerry companies. Unlike them, however, the motto *Statio bene fida carinis—A safe anchorage for ships* was incorrectly rendered *Statio bene fide carinis* in its transfer, which measures 12½ in. high × 14¼ in. wide and is reproduced. This is not altogether surprising; at least one heraldic authority gives *fide* instead of *fida* in the motto of Cork.

Incorporated in 1846, the Cork, Blackrock & Passage was unusual in two respects. It was originally a 5 ft. 3 in. gauge line, opened to Passage in 1850. When it was extended to Crosshaven it was decided to build the new line and convert the existing one to 3 ft. gauge. Secondly, the two miles from Cork to Blackrock, which were doubled at the same time, afforded the only instance of 3 ft. gauge double track in Ireland. The conversion took place in October 1900.

Crosshaven was reached in three instalments, the final one from Carrigaline being opened to traffic on 1st June 1904. The system then amounted to 16 route miles of line. When it became part of the Great Southern it was being operated with 4 locomotives and some 25 coaching vehicles together with 34 goods vehicles.

By this time the effect of bus competition over the shorter route by road between Cork and Crosshaven was being increasingly felt and the double line section was reduced to single track in 1927. Then the Monks-town–Crosshaven section was closed in June 1932 and on 19th September of the same year the last trains ran on the remaining section. The four locomotives were given a reprieve by being transferred to the Cavan & Leitrim section of the Great Southern.

Dublin, Wicklow & Wexford device
Metro-Cammell Collection

Dublin & South Eastern Railway

This company was originally incorporated in 1846 as the *Waterford, Wexford, Wicklow & Dublin*. It got its priorities right in 1860 when it changed its name to *Dublin, Wicklow & Wexford*, having reached Wicklow from Dublin in 1856. It was opened to Wexford in 1872, New Ross in 1887, Waterford in 1904 and assumed the title *Dublin & South Eastern* at the beginning of 1907. With its lease in 1856 of the Dublin & Kingstown, the first public railway in Ireland, opened as early as 17th December 1834, the company was alone in having two terminals in the capital, Westland Row and Harcourt Street. The total route mileage owned, leased or worked was 156.

As the Dublin, Wicklow & Wexford one of the most colourful of all Irish railway armorial devices was adopted. The shield was quartered by Wicklow (top left); the three *lymphads flammant* (heraldic ships on fire) of the town of Wexford (top right); the stag and greyhound 'in full course towards the *sinister*' of New Ross (bottom left); and the three English lions (King John granted its charter) and three ships of seafaring Waterford (bottom right). The escutcheon in the centre carried the three burning castles of Dublin. Overall the transfer measures $10\frac{3}{4}$ in. wide $\times$ $13\frac{3}{8}$ in. high. No alterations in the colours, design or dimensions were effected when the company's name was changed. The style of lettering of the new title in the garter was exactly the same as before.

Both before and after 1907 the device was displayed in the conventional position, below the waistline, on the coaching stock, which was given a crimson lake exterior finish. On the locomotives the usual place for it was high up on the cab side sheets of both tender and tank engines, although there were a few exceptions. Before the 1914–1918 war, when the locomotive livery was crimson lake too, a monogram of the company's initials was also sometimes applied to tender and bunker side sheets. The final locomotive livery was black, picked out with red bands lined gold, and the engines themselves were amongst the best-looking in Ireland.

The contribution of the Dublin & South Eastern to the Great Southern included 64 locomotives, 268 coaching vehicles and 1,063 merchandise and mineral vehicles.

Great Southern & Western Railway

For many years the largest railway company in Ireland, the Great Southern & Western dated back to 1844, when it was incorporated to build a line from Dublin to Cashel, afterwards to Cork. The first section, from Dublin to Carlow, a distance of $56\frac{1}{2}$ miles, was opened on 4th August 1846 and the line thence to Cork was brought into use on 29th October 1849.

From 1860 onwards the expansion of the company, either by new construction or take over, continued apace. Before the end of the century its metals extended southwards to Tullow, Palace East, Rosslare Harbour and Waterford, south westwards to Cork, Kenmare, Valentia and Tralee and westwards to Athlone, Banagher and Birdhill. The biggest amalgamations took place in 1900, when the Waterford & Central Ireland and Waterford, Limerick & Western Railways added 415 route miles to the system. When the Great Southern & Western played the lead in the Irish railway grouping of 1925 it owned some 329 locomotives, 900 coaching vehicles and over 7,800 freight vehicles, together with a small chain of hotels.

It was not the practice to embellish the locomotives with any heraldic device but the coaches, which were given a purple lake exterior finish, were often ornamented with the company's colourful coat of arms, the transfer of which measures $12\frac{3}{4}$ in. wide $\times$ $13\frac{3}{4}$ in. high over black shading. The design embodies the arms of Dublin (top left), a castle of three towers, with a lion in the foreground, to denote Kilkenny (top right) part of the arms of Limerick (bottom left) and the arms of Cork.

Of the several railways absorbed by the Great Southern & Western only the Waterford, Limerick & Western is known to have displayed a coat of arms transfer on its locomotives and coaches, which wore a rich livery of crimson lake, lined-out in gold, except for the goods engines, which were painted black, lined-out in red. It measures $10\frac{1}{2}$ in. wide $\times$ 12 in. high over black shading and is extremely rare. There is an equally rare variant, differing only in respect of the background colour of the garter, which is emerald green.

Its design is unusual in that the shield is divided into three parts instead of the customary four quarters and, at the same time, includes an escutcheon. On the left Waterford is represented by three lions and three ships (the latter being displayed vertically, whereas on the Dublin & South Eastern emblem they are shown horizontally); on the right is denoted part of the Limerick arms by a structure markedly different from that appearing on the Great Southern & Western device; and at the base is represented Clonmel, with a stag pursued by greyhounds across a three-arched bridge (which should consist of five arches) with three fishes *naiant* (swimming) in the base, a scene rather similar to that depicted on the New Ross arms. The escutcheon portrays a tolerably good representation of the company's 4-4-0 express engine *Jubilee*, unexpectedly finished in a *green* livery.

Incorporated in 1845 as the Waterford & Limerick to build a line between the two places in its title, the first section was opened between Limerick and Tipperary on 9th May 1848. The wider title was assumed in 1895, when the lines owned or worked extended from Waterford, via Limerick and Claremorris, to Sligo, with branches to Killaloe, Foynes and Tralee. The Clonmel–Thurles line was worked on behalf of the Board of Trade. The final route mileage was 350, over which was operated a fleet of 58 locomotives, 179 coaching vehicles and 1,350 freight vehicles.

Midland Great Western Railway

Traversing the waist of Ireland with a main line of $126\frac{1}{2}$ miles from Dublin to Galway, and thence to Clifden, the Midland Great Western, often referred to as the Midland, was incorporated in 1845. Its first section, from the handsome, if somewhat out-of-the-way, Broadstone terminus in Dublin to Enfield was opened on 28th June 1847. Mullingar was reached in 1848 and Galway in 1851.

Of the several branches eventually built, those from Mullingar via Longford to Sligo (84½ miles) and from Athlone to Westport (82¾ miles) ranked almost of equal importance with the main line. On the former there were connexions with two other systems, the erstwhile Waterford, Limerick & Western and the Sligo, Leitrim & Northern Counties, at Collooney, a place with 600 inhabitants lavishly endowed with three railway stations! The line from Athlone to Westport, and a branch to Ballina, were built by the Great Northern & Western Railway, which was leased by the Midland in 1870 and amalgamated with it twenty years later. The route mileage of the system, owned, leased or worked, eventually totalled 538, making it the third longest in Ireland.

A transfer of the company's armorial device, 10¼ in. wide × 11¾ in. high, was displayed on some of the locomotives (all of which were named at one time) and coaching stock. It was comprised of the arms of Dublin in the first and fourth quarters, of the extinct arms of Lord Blayney of Castle Blayney, County Monaghan in the second and of the arms of the town of Longford in the third. The reason for the inclusion of the Blayney device is obscure, for no connexion between the company and the Blayney family can be established and its metals did not penetrate into County Monaghan.

In no case were the original heraldic colours perpetuated! The three burning castles of Dublin should have been shown on a blue field; the three nag's heads of Blayney should have been of silver and *erased* (namely with jagged edges to the cut and not *couped* as depicted) on a black field; and the griffins and boars of Longford should have been of blue and of silver on ermine and red fields respectively. But it was not altogether unusual for a railway to make such changes to suit its own purpose. This has already been demonstrated by the way the castle in part of the Limerick arms was differently portrayed in the Waterford, Limerick & Western and Great Southern & Western devices.

The Royal blue, lined black and gold, locomotives and coaches (the latter having white upper panels) of a Midland Great Western express at the turn of the century, with the arms emblazoned on the leading splasher of the engine and twice below the waist of each coach, must have presented a beautiful sight. This livery did not last for many years, however, reverting around 1908 to the previous style of grass green, lined black and white for the engines and brown for the coaches.

When the company's 139 locomotives, 399 passenger train vehicles and

Cork, Bandon & South Coast
BRB Collection

Cork, Blackrock & Passage

Dublin & South Eastern

PLATE 19

Great Southern & Western

Midland Great Western

Waterford, Limerick & Western
W. H. D. Faulkner Collection

PLATE 20

2,861 goods train vehicles were taken over by the Great Southern Railways a more sombre livery was in use, namely black for the locomotives (red lining-out being conceded for the passenger engines) and lake, picked out in straw and vermilion, for the coaching stock.

Tralee & Dingle monogram

Tralee & Dingle nickel uniform button (24mm dia)
David Swan Collection

Tralee & Dingle Light Railway

One of the most remote and most Irish parts of Ireland, the Dingle peninsula in western County Kerry, which is magnificently endowed with cliff and mountain scenery, was once served by the Tralee & Dingle Light Railway. Whether it was the remoteness or the scenery or the magic of the name, or something of all three, the line had an irresistible attraction for some railway enthusiasts.

It was incorporated in 1888 and built 3 ft. gauge tracks, often beside the road, between the places in its title, with a branch to Castlegregory, which were opened for traffic on 31st March 1891. The total route mileage was 38, some of it as steeply graded as 1 in 29 to 1 in 40.

At its zenith the Tralee & Dingle owned 8 locomotives, 21 passenger vehicles and 78 goods vehicles, but it never indulged in an armorial device as did some of its narrow gauge contemporaries elsewhere. Tearnes did, however, supply an enormous garter-cum-monogram transfer in 1890 for the coaching stock. It was the largest ever produced for a British railway and measures no less than 27 in. wide by 18 in. high. The monogram is gilt, as is the edging and ornamentation of the plain garter, which is vermilion.

See supplement p. 11

Staff uniform buttons, which were nickel, were embossed with a shamrock surrounded with the name of the railway.

On 17th April 1939, when the line was part of Great Southern Railways, passenger traffic ceased and the Castlegregory branch was completely closed. Freight traffic diminished to such an extent that during the last years of the line's existence there were but two trains a month . . . an empty cattle train to Dingle on the last Friday, returning loaded to Tralee the next day! This came to an end on 28th June 1953.

Of the four engines then remaining two were scrapped and the others were given a new lease of life on West Clare metals, to which fourteen of the coaching vehicles had been transferred after passenger services ceased.

Waterford & Tramore Railway

Incorporated in 1851 for a railway connecting the two places in its title, the Waterford & Tramore was opened on 5th September 1853. It was built to the standard Irish gauge of 5 ft. 3 in. but throughout its life of more than 107 years its $7\frac{1}{4}$ miles of line remained physically isolated from the rest of the system, even after it had become part of the Great Southern in 1925. Not until this had taken place was a start made to equip its rolling stock with continuous vacuum brakes.

To work the line some 4 locomotives, 21 coaching vehicles and 12 freight vehicles sufficed in pre-Great Southern days. Locomotives were resplendent in brass and copper, the livery being light green with black ands edged vermilion for the body and brown for the frames. Coaches were four-wheeled and six-wheeled, and as the stations at Waterford Manor) and Tramore were on the west side of the line coach doors were only provided on that side! Another unusual practice was to paint the coaches according to class; the firsts were finished in dark blue with white lining and the thirds dark red with black lining.

Waterford & Tramore garter

The company indulged in no coat of arms and contented itself with an orthodox garter transfer for the coaches. Into this the number was inserted, the firsts and thirds being numbered separately. This transfer measures $9\frac{1}{4}$ in. wide $\times$ $11\frac{3}{4}$ in. high. It embodies the usual gilt edging and ornamentation to the red garter, the gilt lettering on which is shaded black.

Diesel rail cars replaced steam traction and goods train services ceased towards the end of 1954. The line managed to exist for another six years, being closed down on the last day of 1960.

West Clare Railway

Nothing could be more Irish than the armorial device of the West Clare
Railway, whose early idiosyncrasies the late Percy French, one time
concert artist, mocked in his comic ballad *Are ye right there, Michael?* A
gilt harp encircled by an emerald green garter, gilt-edged with gilt buckle
and ornaments, with gilt lettering having green inner shading and black
outer shading, formed its attractive emblem. The transfer was worn by
locomotives and carriages and measures $12\frac{1}{4}$ in. wide × $14\frac{3}{4}$ in. high
over black shading.

The West Clare was registered in 1883, taking advantage of the Tramways Act of that year. It was built to the 3 ft. gauge and was opened from
Ennis, on the Limerick–Athenry line of the Waterford, Limerick &
Western, to the small Atlantic coast resort of Miltown Malbay, a distance
of 27 miles, on 2nd July 1887.

West Clare garter

By this time the South Clare Railways had been formed to extend the
line southwards to Kilkee, another coastal resort, with a branch from
Moyasta Junction to Kilrush and Cappa Pier on the river Shannon

Moyasta Junction was to be triangular so that trains could run direct between Kilrush and Kilkee; indeed, this was the first section to be opened and it is known that two special trains for an election meeting were operated between these places on 3rd July 1892, before the Board of Trade inspection!

South Clare garter

The Cappa Pier–Kilrush–Kilkee section was officially opened to the public on the 3rd of the following month and on 23rd December 1892 through services began between Ennis and Kilrush, which was regarded as the main line. Total route mileage of the South Clare was 26.

From the outset the West Clare worked the South Clare. The locomotives and rolling stock of the two companies were operated as for one system, although for several years South Clare ownership of some units was denoted by the display of an armorial device which, save for the title, was identical in every respect with that of the West Clare.

The West and South Clare Railways became the Clare section of the Great Southern and the suffix 'C' was added to the running numbers of the 9 locomotives, 35 coaching vehicles and 170 goods vehicles. The little system eventually passed to the ownership of Coras Iompair Eireann, under whose auspices diesel traction was introduced in 1950.

When its last trains ran on 31st January 1961 it had become the sole survivor of the narrow gauge in Ireland, which had once totalled some 570 miles of line.

Great Southern device

Great Southern Railways

With the creation of the Irish Free State a Commission was set up to examine the railway situation generally, as a consequence of which the decision was taken to merge all the railways, save only those which crossed the border with Northern Ireland, to achieve much needed economies in working. With a deadline of 31st August 1924 the railway companies were encouraged to initiate a process of voluntary amalgamation whilst preparation of the Bill was taken in hand.

This rather unusual way of achieving unification resulted in its consummation in two stages. A voluntary merger of the Great Southern & Western and Cork, Bandon & South Coast, joined by the Midland Great Western, led to the registration of the *Great Southern Railway* in November 1924. The passage of the Irish Railways Act of that year compelled the other companies to join in, and the total amalgamation became effective as from 1st January 1925 under the title *Great Southern Railways*.

The new company adapted the Great Southern & Western armorial device, making but one alteration to it apart from the change of title.

Kilkenny, in the second quarter, was displaced by a black ship, riding on green natural water, to represent Galway. The transfer made by Tearnes for the ornamentation of coaching stock was otherwise identical with that produced for the Great Southern & Western both as regards colour and size.

Staff uniform buttons closely resembled those of the Tralee & Dingle. Made of nickel, they were embossed with a shamrock surrounded by the company's title.

Great Southern nickel uniform button (25mm dia)
David Swan Collection

PART EIGHT

Other Railways in the British Isles

Ballycastle Railway

Connecting Ballymoney, on the Belfast & Northern Counties London-derry–Belfast main line, with the resort of Ballycastle, on the coast of Antrim, the 3 ft. gauge Ballycastle Railway was incorporated in 1878. It was opened on 18th October 1880, the Belfast & Northern Counties having subscribed £18,000 towards the capital of the company.

The Rev. Sir Frederick Boyd, who succeeded his nephew, was the first Chairman of the Ballycastle, and themes from the arms of his and other branches of the Boyd family entirely made up the armorial device of the railway. A circular transfer 11 in. in diameter, a near replica of the seal, was produced by Tearnes, but no specimen can be traced. The key plate, somewhat damaged, has fortunately survived, however, and this is reproduced.

Key plate of Ballycastle device
W. H. D. Faulkner Collection

By the end of the first world war the fortunes of the company had reached such a low ebb that a Railway Commission for Northern Ireland suggested its absorption by the Midland in 1922. This idea fell on stony ground and, as the LMS evinced no enthusiasm either when approached two years later, the 16¼ mile line was closed on 4th April 1924. The LMS thereupon had second thoughts, obtained sanction to add the line to it Northern Counties Committee and reopened it on 11th August of the same year. It was closed for the second and last time on 3rd July 1950

Belfast & County Down Railway

Incorporated in 1846 to build a line from Belfast to Downpatrick, with branches to Holywood, Donaghadee and Bangor, the first section of the Belfast & County Down was opened to Holywood two years later. Down patrick was reached in 1859, Donaghadee in 1861, Bangor in 1865 and Newcastle in 1869. Branches were also built to Ballynahinch, Ardglass and Castlewellan; at the latter place an end-on junction was effected with the Great Northern, with which it was also physically connected in Belfast. The total route mileage of line was 80.

The company's armorial device was very impressive and the transfer which was made of it measured no less than 18 in. wide × 13½ in. high; a small version 4⅛ in. wide × 3 in. high was also printed. Taken from the Belfast arms were the crest, a sea horse *gorged* with a mural crown, and the supporters, a wolf ducally *gorged* and chained in gold, and a sea horse, again *gorged* with a mural crown. The shield of Belfast is the righthand one of the pair. Centrally in the upper part is a *pile vair*, an inverted triangle of bellshaped *argent* and *azure* fur, and in the lefthand top corner is a *canton*—a small quarter—containing a bell. A two-masted sailing ship on natural water and the motto *Pro tanto quid retribuamus—What return can we make for so much?* completes the design.

Granted to the City by the Ulster King of Arms in 1890, the Belfast achievement is, in fact, of considerable antiquity, being almost identical with the seal of Henry le Squire, Sovereign of the town 1635–1636 and 1639. At that time he was agent to the Lord Edward Chichester, from whose arms the wolf and *pile vair* were derived. The bell and fast sailing ship are not, by the way, a play on the word Belfast, but have their origin in merchants' signs.

On the left of the Belfast shield is the arms of County Down. Here the upper part is occupied by a couple of spinning jennies which, together with the two shuttles and the wheatsheaf between them, denote the rural industries of the county. At the base is a smaller version of the Belfast sailing ship and, beneath it, the motto *Industria*.

The transfer ornamented the crimson lake, yellow lined coaches and many of the dark green locomotives. On the latter it occupied a position high up on the cab side sheets of both tender and tank engines as well as the more customary position centrally on the tender sides. There were some 30 locomotives and a stock of about 200 passenger vehicles and 700 goods vehicles.

The Belfast & County Down became part of the Ulster Transport Authority in 1948. Today the last testimony to a once thriving little system is the line from Belfast to Bangor, now operated by diesel trains in the livery of Northern Ireland Railways.

Emblem of the Bideford, Westward Ho! & Appledore

Bideford, Westward Ho! & Appledore Railway

A standard gauge line, physically unconnected with any other railway, the Bideford, Westward Ho! & Appledore was fated to survive actively for less than sixteen years. Authorised in 1896, after an abortive start thirty years earlier, it was opened from Bideford to Northam on 24th April 1901, extended to Appledore on 1st May 1908 and closed on 28th April 1917, when its three 2-4-2 tank locomotives and permanent way were requisitioned by the Government for war purposes. No attempt to reopen the line was made when hostilities ended.

Six handsome polished teak bogie coaches built at Bristol—two thirds and four composites—with end entrances and balconies giving them a distinctly American appearance, were sufficient for the business of the line. Centrally each side was a circular device consisting of an emblem representing Bideford (superseded by a coat of arms granted in 1937) surrounded by the company's title.

Whether the emblem was transferred or, more likely, handpainted i
not known. No specimen appears to have survived and the accompanying
black and white reproduction of it is based upon information supplied b
the Town Clerk of Bideford and contemporary photographs in th
author's collection.

Bishops Castle painted garter

Bishops Castle Railway

'A journey over it was in itself an education in railway history. N
telegraph or telephone, just as in the early days of railways, when nobod
knew where a train might be until it arrived; a track laid with rails an
chairs which in some cases were dated 1865 and ballasted with earth
semaphores of antique pattern, dropping into the post for "all clear" an
appearing to be operated on no principle at all. . . .' Thus and more wrot
the late much travelled T. R. Perkins in *The Railway Magazine* about th
Bishops Castle Railway after its closure on 20th April 1935.

It had been incorporated in 1863 and the only part of its authorise
lines to be built was that from Craven Arms to Lydham Heath and thenc
to Bishops Castle, a total length of 9½ miles, which was opened on 1
February 1866. Within a year the Bishops Castle was in the hands of
Receiver, and there it remained for the rest of its life. It is a wonder th
it lasted as long as it did.

The coaching stock was a miscellany of four- and six-wheeled mid-Victorian antiquities originating from the Brecon & Merthyr, Hull & Barnsley and other lines. Their livery was dark chocolate.

Coach No. 1, an ex-North Western four-wheeled composite, and other chain brake vehicles like it, dispayed their number in gilt shaded red, within a garter edged, ornamented and lettered in gilt, similarly shaded. The emblem measured 8 in. wide × 10 in. high, the illustration being of a full size reproduction hand-painted for the author by A. M. Gunn.

Bluebell Railway

Under powers given in 1877 to a private concern, which was vested in the London, Brighton & South Coast in the following year, the Lewes & East Grinstead Railway came into being. It ran from Culver junction, near Barcombe, to East Grinstead (opened on 1st August 1882), with a branch from Horsted Keynes to Haywards Heath on the main line (opened on 3rd September 1883). It became known as the 'Bluebell' line.

Unfortunately it largely duplicated existing routes and served an essentially rural area. The section between Culver junction and Horsted Keynes was closed completely by British Railways in March 1958 and would have gone into oblivion but for the initiative of the Bluebell Railway Preservation Society, who were determined to ensure that it did not. By their efforts the 4½ miles of line between Sheffield Park and Horsted Keynes was acquired from its owners. An Order converting it into a Light Railway was obtained by the British Transport Commission from the Minister of Transport on 15th June 1960 and, following a visit by the latter's Inspecting Officer on 9th July, a further order transferred it to the Bluebell Railway Ltd.

Bluebell device
Photo: K. D. Chown

Operated with vintage steam locomotives and rolling stock, the Bluebell has gone from strength to strength. It celebrated its tenth anniversary by evolving a neat heraldic device which perhaps one day will adorn some of its equipment.

The first quarter of the shield, illustrated, depicts the crest of the Holroyd family, Earls of Sheffield, which has been obsolete from about 1903. It is from the former family seat of Sheffield Park that Sheffield Park station, now headquarters of the Bluebell Railway, takes its name, although in fact it is in Fletching. In the second quarter are the arms of Lewes and in the next those of East Grinstead Urban District, with the approval of both. Lastly, in the fourth quarter, are the arms of the Norman family of Cahaignes, obsolete for some 400 years, from which Horsted Keynes ('House of Caynes') derives its name.

As a motto, *Floreat vapor*, which may be translated *May Steam flourish*, gives the final touch to a well thought out device.

Campbeltown & Macrihanish Light Railway

If one excludes the 4 ft. gauge 6½ miles long underground electric line of Glasgow Corporation Transport, still going strong, the only narrow gauge metals in Scotland were those of the 2 ft. 3 in. gauge Campbeltown & Macrihanish Light Railway, of the same mileage, which straddled Kintyre in Argyll.

Opened in 1877 for coal traffic, it was extended and adapted for passenger traffic in 1906. The first timetable in *Bradshaw* showed three trains daily each way, these being doubled up on Saturdays, for which six olive green and cream 43 ft. 6 in. bogie cars sufficed.

The two locomotives, named *Argyll* and *Atlantic*, which were responsible for practically the whole of the passenger services during the lifetime of the company, were 0-6-2 tanks built by Andrew Barclay. They wore an olive green livery, embellished at the leading end of each side tank by a distinctive armorial device of which, fortunately, a specimen has been preserved in the British Railways Board Collection.

Encircled within a garter bearing the company's title, it consists of a crest depicting a 4-4-0 tender engine, *sans* tender, of an indeterminate type which the line never possessed! Beneath it, the shield was a not altogether correct replica of part of the armorial bearings of the Royal Burgh of Campbeltown.

The yellow castle on a red field in the first quarter (which should be in gold and green) denotes the old castle of the Macdonalds which stood for centuries on Castle hill, the colours being those of the ancient Dalriodic kings who made their capital in Kintyre. The *gyronny* in black and gold n the second quarter and gold ship (which should be black) in the third quarter are respectively the cognisance of the Campbells and the Galley of Lorne, both being borrowed from the arms of the Argyll family and intended as a compliment to the first Duke, who gave the Burgh its Charter. The fourth quarter, a red *fretty* on a putty background (which should be black on white) is the arms of the Tollemaches in Suffolk and commemor- ates the long and intimate association of Elizabeth Tollemache, first Duchess of Argyll, with the Burgh. The design has an overall diameter of o$\frac{1}{8}$ in.

Although the Campbeltown & Macrihanish was the most isolated public railway in Britain it was not spared the competition of the ubiquitous motor bus, which was serious enough to bring about the total closure of the line in the latter part of 1931.

Castlederg & Victoria Bridge Tramway

Opened on 11th July 1884, this steam tramway was, in fact, a railway, albeit a light railway. Passengers, mails, goods and livestock were carried over its 7$\frac{1}{4}$ miles of 3 ft. gauge metals alongside public roads between the small market town of Castlederg and Victoria Bridge station on the Strabane–Omagh line of the Great Northern.

And it could boast an heraldic device, now one of the most rare. . . . 'Azure a buckle argent between three boars heads couped or armed and langued gules' describes the shield, which was surmounted by a crest consisting of a thistle and a visiting bee. The arms were those of the Ferguson family.

Sir Robert Ferguson, MP for Derry City, Lieutenant of the County of Londonderry and Deputy Lieutenant of the Counties of Tyrone and Donegal, realising how beneficial light railways would be to Ireland, had sponsored a Bill which resulted in the passage of the 1860 Tramways Act. He had died that same year, when the baronetcy became extinct, but his youngest sister, Elizabeth had married John G. Smyly, Q.C., and their son Major John G. Smyly, who became a large landowner in Tyrone, was one of the first Directors of the tramway company. No doubt he was largely instrumental in getting the Ferguson arms adopted as its device, as a tribute to Sir Robert's pioneer work in light railway development.

The transfer measures 10$\frac{1}{2}$ in. in diameter and was displayed on the tank sides of the locomotives, which wore a brick red (later chocolate) livery, and passenger coaches alike. All rolling stock was equipped with air brakes; indeed the company was the first in Ireland to introduce Westinghouse brakes.

By 1925 bus competition was making such inroads that alternative forms of traction—a Fordson rail motor running on paraffin and a diesel locomotive—were tried out, but without marked success. At the beginning of a Northern Ireland railway strike on 31st January 1933 the company's services ceased and were never resumed. The 3 locomotives, 5 coaches and 29 goods vehicles were sold by auction in the following year.

Keyplate of Jersey Railways device
W. H. D. Faulkner Collection

Jersey Railways gilt uniform button
(16mm dia)
David Swan Collection

Railways in the Channel Islands

Public railways in the largest of the Channel Islands date back to 1870 when Jersey Railways Ltd formally opened its standard gauge line from St Helier to St Aubin on 25th October of that year. A 3 ft. 6 in. gauge extension on to Corbiere was brought into use on 1st September 1885 and the St Helier–St Aubin section converted to that gauge at the same time. Jersey Railways & Tramways Ltd, which was registered as a company on 18th January 1896, took over the company on that date and continued to operate the line until its closure in 1936.

Tearnes produced an armorial transfer for the original company, but no specimens are known to exist. Its key plate measures 12 in. wide × 13½ in. high and, as will be seen, consists simply of the arms of Jersey enclosed within a garter. Staff uniform buttons were of similar design.

Jersey Railways & Tramways Ltd employed the somewhat prosaic monogram illustrated and there is no evidence that it indulged in any other insignia.

Belfast & County Down

Castlederg & Victoria Bridge

Clogher Valley

Great Northern (Ireland)

PLATE 21

Isle of Man 1st device
BRB Collection

Isle of Man 2nd device

Isle of Man 3rd device

Manx Northern

PLATE 22

Its neighbour, the Jersey Eastern, was incorporated in 1872, built to the standard gauge and completed in stages from St Helier to Gorey Village in 1873–4; a short extension, to Gorey Pier was opened in 1891. It was closed throughout in 1929 and does not appear to have used an emblem of any kind. *See Supplement p.12*

There were two other railways in the Channel Islands. One was the three mile standard gauge Guernsey Railway from St Peter Port to St Sampson, opened on 9th June 1879, which began as a steam tramway and was converted to an orthodox electric tramway early in 1892. In the previous year Tearnes supplied a simple oval garter for it, $14\frac{3}{4}$ in. wide × $12\frac{1}{2}$ in. high, bearing the legend *Guernsey Railway Company Ltd*. It was closed in 1934.

The other was the little Alderney Railway, a two mile standard gauge Admiralty line which dated from the construction of the famous breakwater, inaugurated in 1847. It ran the length of the breakwater to the quarry at Mannez, was worked by two steam locomotives and, in its time, was one of the rare examples of a state-owned railway in this country before 1948.

Emblem of Jersey Railways & Tramways Ltd
BRB Collection

Clogher Valley Railway

Incorporated in 1883 the Clogher Valley Tramway, as it was then called, was authorised to build 3 ft. gauge tracks from Tynan, on the Belfast—

Cavan line of the Great Northern, to Maguiresbridge, on the same company's Enniskillen–Dundalk line. Interest on its capital was baronially guaranteed by certain districts of the counties of Tyrone and Fermanagh.

The 37 route miles of line were ceremonially opened on 2nd May 1887 at Aughnacloy, the headquarters of the company, when Major Knox Brown, the High Sheriff of Tyrone, poured champagne over locomotive No 1 *Caledon*, before retiring to lunch in the carriage shed with other members of the official party.

Metropolitan Carriage & Wagon Company supplied the whole of the 88 units of rolling stock ordered for the line, all the passenger coaches being bogie vehicles which, with their end platforms and clerestory roofs, had a decided American look about them; they were noteworthy for being amongst the first in the United Kingdom to be steam heated. The six original locomotives were Sharp Stewart 0-4-2 tanks and all were named; some subsequently were ornamented with a monogram.

In 1894 the company changed its title to Clogher Valley Railway, which relieved it of certain Board of Trade obligations. Soon afterwards the accompanying transfer of its heraldic device began to appear centrally on the waists of the crimson red coaches. It measures $10\frac{1}{4}$ in. wide × 12 in. high and is quartered by part of the arms of the Baron O'Neill (top left and bottom right) and the coat of arms of Maguire . . . 'vert a white horse fully caparisoned thereupon a white knight in complete armour, on his helm a plume of ostrich feathers and his right hand brandishing a sword all proper.' The O'Neills were landowners of Co. Tyrone and the Maguires were the Lords of Co. Fermanagh, hence Maguiresbridge, the western terminus of the line. The escutcheon is the arms of Caledon where, as at Fivemiletown, the railway ran down the middle of the main street.

The Clogher Valley was a well equipped line, but never prosperous. Road competition was its downfall and after 1912 it began to incur losses on working. In 1928 it was taken over jointly by the Tyrone and Fermanagh County Councils, who ultimately introduced diesel traction. But the annual deficits continued to mount and the end came in 1941, the last day of which was its last day of operation. Most of its property eventually went under the auctioneer's hammer.

Corris Railway

This slate carrying 2 ft. 3 in. gauge line was incorporated in 1858 as the Corris, Machynlleth & River Dovey Tramroad. It was opened in 1859, or thereabouts, as a horse-cum-gravity operated line, and in 1864 changed its name to *Corris Railway*, at the same time getting authority to use loco-motives. Passenger services began between Machynlleth and Corris in 1883 and were extended to Aberllefenni four years later.

Steam traction was inaugurated early in 1879 with three locomotives. When passenger services began there were sixteen four-wheeled coaches with end balconies, very much like diminutive tramcars; they did not ride well and in 1898 a start was made to mount them in pairs on steel underframes equipped with bogies. In this form they were given an umber brown livery, with yellow lining, lettering and numbering, a similar style having been adopted for the locomotives.

Corris garter

At the same time a transfer emblem $14\frac{5}{8}$ in. wide $\times$ $12\frac{1}{2}$ in. high over black shading was applied to the rebuilt coaches. It consisted of a sky blue garter, shaded Royal blue, with gilt edging, ornamentation and lettering, the last-named being shaded black. Tearnes printed the first supply in February 1899 and specimens are to be seen today on the Corris coach which eventually migrated to the Talyllyn Railway.

Staff uniform buttons were embossed with the feathers of the Prince of Wales, a practice adopted by some other Welsh lines.

In 1930 the Corris was bought by the Great Western and the passenger traffic was relinquished entirely to buses at the end of that year. But goods and mineral services were continued until working losses and the serious effects of flooding in the Dovey on more than one occasion caused the last trains to run on 20th August 1948.

Two of the locomotives, Nos 3 and 4, together with some of the wagons, a van and the coach mentioned were transferred to the Talyllyn, where they have since put in yeoman work.

Dart Valley Railway

An abortive attempt in the 1840s to build a railway from Ashburton to the South Devon Railway at Newton Abbot was succeeded in 1864 by the incorporation of the ponderously entitled Buckfastleigh, Totnes & South Devon Railway. In the following year the company was authorised to extend to Ashburton, making a total of some 9 route miles. Built to Brunel's extravagant broad gauge of 7 ft. o¼ in., it was opened throughout on 1st May 1872 and worked by the impoverished South Devon. The take-over of the latter by the Great Western was legalised in 1878, but the BT & SD was not absorbed until 1897. By this time the gauge had been converted to standard.

Decline in traffic led to the withdrawal of passenger services on 3rd November 1958 and of the freight services on 10th September 1962. In less than three weeks, however, it was announced that a group of businessmen planned to re-open the line and in due course the Dart Valley Light Railway Co Ltd was formed for the purpose. A Light Railway Order was granted on 1st April 1969 and the first public passenger trains began running again four days later between Buckfastleigh and Staverton Bridge, pending the building of a new station at Totnes Riverside.

Dart Valley painted device
R. J. S. Saunders Collection

A neat heraldic device has been adopted by the new company and is reproduced. It measures 8½ in. wide × 8 in. high and quarters the arms of London and Bristol with those of Ashburton (top right) and Totnes (bottom left). Ashburton is denoted by a yellow church with dark blue door and roofs; above it are a gilt sun, a blue cloud and a blue outlined moon. This is derived from a 14th century seal which embodied the chapel of the Chantry of St Lawrence, founded by Bishop Stapleton of Exeter in 1314. Totnes is represented by a castle, also in yellow, with dark blue roofs to its twin towers, which are flanked by dark blue flags (which should be keys) bearing white crosses. The background of Bristol is the customary red and that of the other quarters is white (strictly speaking the background of Totnes should be black). The shield has a gilt outline and the title is displayed in blue lettering on a blue-edged white riband shaded greyish blue.

The emblem is employed on stationery and publicity material.

Fairbourne device

Fairbourne Railway

The Fairbourne is one of the oldest established 15 in. gauge passenger carrying lines in the British Isles. It began in 1890 as a 2 ft. gauge tramway, running from Fairbourne station of the Cambrian Railways for a distance of two miles to Penrhyn Point, whence a ferry operates across the Mawddach estuary to Barmouth. Conversion to 15 in. gauge, with the existing materials, took place in 1916 under the auspices of the Bassett—Lowke Ltd associate firm Narrow Gauge Railways Ltd.

Today the line is controlled by Fairbourne Railway Ltd, the leading light of which is J. C. Wilkins, a Midlands industrialist. Motive power consists of both steam and internal combustion locomotives, some ten in all, of which two handsome freelance 2-4-2 tender engines *Katie* and *Sian* were built as recently as 1956 and 1963. There are also two dozen passenger cars and a few wagons.

The livery of most of the locomotives and coach units is middle Brunswick green, usually adorned with the company's emblem illustrated. A genial looking red Welsh dragon is the central feature of this neat little circular device of 6 in. diameter. The background consists of blue and white heraldic sea, a greensward and a grey mountain superimposed upon the spokes of a wheel, behind which is a blue sky and grey clouds shot with the orange of a rising sun. The tyre of the wheel, which is grey, acts as an encircling band and carries the title of the railway in gilt letters, shaded black.

Festiniog Railway

Pioneer of the 1 ft. 11½ in. gauge in Great Britain, the Festiniog was incorporated as long ago as 1832 to build a railway from Portmadoc to various slate quarries near Festiniog, some 14 miles. It was opened with ceremony on 20th April 1836. With the exception of a cable operated incline (which was soon replaced by a tunnel) and the level section across the Traeth Mawr embankment at Portmadoc, the whole line was on a falling gradient. Loaded slate wagons, with special wagons carrying horses at the tail end, went down from the quarries by gravity and were hauled back empty by the horses!

Steam traction was introduced in 1863, the first two engines being embellished with the Prince of Wales' feathers hand-painted on each side centrally above the nameplates. The Royal cipher became the emblem of the railway. It was embossed on the metal buttons of the staff uniforms and was adopted as a device for the liberal adornment of locomotives and carriages when a transfer design was produced by Tearnes *circa* 1870.

It measures 6¼ in. wide × 10 in. high over brown shading which was changed to black when a new supply was ordered in 1898. The crest, of white feathers shaded grey, issues from a gilt crown studded with red and green jewels. A green riband, gilt bordered, carries the motto *Ich Dien* in gilt letters. The garter is white, shaded red and edged and ornamented in gilt, and carries the title in blue letters.

Declining slate and passenger traffic eventually led first to the abandonment of passenger services in 1939 and then to the total closure of the line seven years later. Its revival was due to the timely intervention of Alan Pegler who bought up the controlling shares so that the railway

Festiniog device

Festiniog in carpet

could be operated once again, this time with the assistance of the voluntarily supported Festiniog Railway Society. The actual date of the take-over was 24th June 1954.

Since then the onerous task of restoring and renewing track, locomotives and rolling stock has proceeded apace and the line is busy again as far inland as Dduallt. The armorial device of the original company has been retained and has now been embodied in the carpets of 1st class compartments. This is woven in the full colours and looks very striking on a green background.

Foxfield Light Railway

Towards the end of the last century Foxfield colliery, near Dilhorne, in Staffordshire, was brought into use and, in 1893, connected by its own line to the North Staffordshire Railway at Blythe Bridge. It was duly taken over by the National Coal Board and closed as uneconomic in 1965, when it was purchased by Tean Minerals Ltd.

A meeting to discuss the resurrection of the railway was held at Foxfield on 30th October 1966 and from this sprang the Foxfield Light Railway Society, which brought the $3\frac{1}{2}$ miles of line into operation again and owns two of the nine privately owned locomotives working upon it.

Foxfield Light Railway Society stationery device

The stationery of the Society is embellished by a neat black and white emblem. It consists of a locomotive wheel, the tyre of which carries the full title of the Society. Superimposed on the spokes is a shield which bears a Staffordshire knot at the top, a Peckett 0-4-0 saddle tank in the centre and a flying fox at the base.

It is an appropriate design, for the first locomotive to be owned by the Society is one of this type built by Peckett & Sons of Bristol in 1903 for Ebbw Vale Steelworks, and it is not unknown for foxes to be seen running through the fields alongside the line.

Glasgow Corporation Underground arms

Glasgow Corporation Underground

An Act was obtained in 1890 for the construction of a tube railway in Glasgow after two previous attempts had failed. It was to follow a circular route of 6½ miles, consisting of double track laid to the unusual gauge of 4 ft., the trains being cable operated.

Known as the Glasgow Subway, it was opened for traffic on 21st January 1897 and bought by Glasgow Corporation on 1st August 1923 for £381,589, less than a quarter of its first cost. Long overdue electrification, embodying a third rail supplying current at 570 volts, took place during 1936, by which time it had become Britain's last example of cable traction.

The rolling stock consists of 26 motor cars, 24 trailer cars and an electric battery service locomotive. The cars are unique in that they are each finished in two different styles of painting. On the platform (and visible) side they originally flaunted a scarlet and cream livery, the centre panel beneath the windows carrying a transfer of the achievement of the city of Glasgow, which has already been described on page 18. This livery was altered to all over scarlet in 1955. On the offside the cars are painted dull red.

This unusual arrangement is adopted because of other even more unusual features. There are no connexions between the inner and outer tracks and at night the cars are parked end-to-end in the tunnels. In consequence, the cars are never exchanged between one line and another and are never turned! When maintenance is necessary, they are hoisted off the tracks at Govan, where the repair shops are situated.

Odd indeed, but it works.

Glyn Valley Tramway monogram

Glyn Valley Tramway

The Glyn Valley Tramway was not a tramway in the accepted sense of the word but a narrow gauge railway running alongside a road for most of its length. It began as a 2 ft. 4¼ in. gauge horse operated tramway managed by the Shropshire Union Canal and was opened in April 1873 between the canal wharf at Gledrid and slate quarries at Glyn Ceiriog in south east Denbighshire, a distance of some 8½ miles. Passenger services started in 1874 and were abandoned twelve years later.

By this time the canal company had surrendered management to the tramway company and in 1885 the latter obtained Parliamentary sanction to extend the line at its western end towards Tregeiriog to tap granite and chinastone quarries, to modify the eastern end so as to terminate alongside the Great Western Railway at Chirk, and to introduce steam traction.

This was all accomplished by 1888, including alteration of gauge to 2 ft. 4½ in., goods and mineral traffic being steam operated from July. Public pressure led to the restoration of passenger services three years later.

Middle green was originally adopted as the external finish of the 3 locomotives, 12 coaches (all 4-wheeled) and 238 wagons and vans in early steam days, the coaches having buff upper panels. No armorial device was in use, but Tearnes produced the monogram-cum-garter transfer illustrated. It measures 15¼ in. wide × 11½ in. high, the plain vermilion garter with its gilt edging and ornamentation, shaded black, surrounding the gilt initials. It stood out well on the green background of the coaches.

Buses and lorries eventually killed the Glyn Valley. Passenger services ceased on 1st April 1933 and on 6th July two years later the line was closed to all traffic. In the ensuing disposal of equipment the coaches, minus their frames and wheels, suffered the indignity of being sold as outhouses. Two of them were subsequently recovered and in 1958, lovingly restored with the GVT insignia on their sides, were put into service as 1st class coaches on the 2 ft. 3 in. gauge Talyllyn Railway in Merionethshire.

Great Northern Railway (Ireland)

Two of the oldest railways in Ireland, the Ulster and the Dublin & Drogheda, which were both incorporated in 1836, were amongst the ancestors of the Great Northern, for many years one of the finest lines in the country. The first named was opened between Belfast and Lisburn in 1839, reaching Armagh nine years later; the second, between the places in its title, in 1844. The two railways were linked by the Dublin & Belfast Junction between Drogheda and Portadown when the Boyne was bridged, temporarily at first, in 1853.

In 1875 the Dublin & Drogheda and the Dublin & Belfast Junction united to become the Northern of Ireland. This set the ball rolling and at the beginning of 1876 the Irish North Western became part of the Northern. Finally, on 1st April 1876, the *Great Northern of Ireland Railway*, to give the legal title, was incorporated by the fusion of the Northern with the Ulster. By new construction and further amalgamations the Great Northern eventually ranked as the second largest in Ireland before the grouping of Irish railways took place in 1925. In 1948 it owned 709 miles of 5 ft. 3 in. gauge track, 150 locomotives, 9 diesel rail cars, 507 coaching vehicles and 5,687 freight vehicles.

For many years its locomotives and coaches and, more recently, other passenger vehicles such as railbuses and single and double decked buses, have been adorned by its distinctive heraldic device. This, it will be observed, quarters the arms of Dublin, Londonderry, Enniskillen and Belfast, upon which is superimposed an escutcheon carrying the Red Hand of Ulster, a left hand and not a right hand, as is to be seen on the Ulster Transport Authority coat of arms.

Great Northern of Ireland gilt uniform button (25mm dia)
David Swan Collection

Dublin (top left) and Belfast (bottom right) have been dealt with elsewhere in these pages. Londonderry (top right) is of interest because its upper half is made up of part of the arms of London with the Irish harp in the middle of the cross of St George. Beneath it a skeleton sits on a stone or mound beside a castle; this is believed to be an allusion to Sir Cahir O'Doherty, who destroyed Derry in 1608 and is supposed to have starved to death in his castle at Buncrana. The arms of Enniskillen (bottom left) are a reproduction of the Castle of Enniskillen.

The transfer of this device was made in three sizes. The largest, 18 in. wide × 20 in. high, was to be seen on locomotive tenders; the inter-mediate, $11\frac{1}{8}$ in. wide × $13\frac{1}{2}$ in. high, on coaches and buses; and the smallest, $8\frac{1}{4}$ in. wide × $9\frac{7}{8}$ in. high, on locomotive coupled wheel splashers. Green, of a similar shade to that of the Great Northern of England, was the locomotive livery for many years before 1912, when black, lined red began to take its place. Sky blue, with black bands, and white edging was introduced for passenger locomotives in 1935. The livery of the coaches was varnished mahogany, lined gold and blue, and an orange-brown colour to match was adopted for steel panelled stock. All bore the coat of arms.

In 1953, by Acts of Parliament passed by the governments of Northern Ireland and the Republic of Ireland, the company was acquired jointly by them both and rechristened *Great Northern Railway Board*. Its armorial device survived this political expediency, unaltered save for the amended title, but the end could not be far away. This came on 1st October 1958, when the undertaking was divided between Coras Iompair Eireann and the Ulster Transport Authority.

Great Northern Railway Board device

Railways in the Isle of Man

The first Manx railway did not come into operation until 2nd July 1873, when the 3 ft. gauge Douglas–Peel line of the Isle of Man Railway was opened to the public. The Port Erin line was brought into use a year later and in 1878 the Manx Northern Railway was registered to build a line from St Johns to Ramsey, duly opened on 23rd September 1879. Working together in close harmony, the Isle of Man took over the operation of the Manx Northern early in 1904 and in April of the following year the latter ceased to exist as a separate concern. The route mileage of the combined railways was 46¼.

Traffic remained buoyant until the early 1950s, when a decline which set in ultimately brought about the closure of the system on 13th November

227

1965. Subsequently, a group of businessmen leased the railway and it was formally reopened on 3rd June 1967.

Three armorial devices have been used by the Isle of Man Railway and these are illustrated (Plate 22). The second and third designs (each measuring 10¾ in. wide × 13 in. high) are shown on the crimson red which, with cream, was adopted as the coach livery in 1950. Both embody the three-legged Manx emblem and good representations of 2-4-0T engines which work the line. In the second design, which was first printed in 1905, the locomotive was drawn from a photograph of No 6 *Peveril*; the third design features No 16 *Mannin*, which was built for the line in 1926.

Two odd features are to be seen in the rare transfer of the Manx Northern device, portrayed on the coach livery, which was brown with cream upper panels. These are the inclusion of a 2-4-0 tender locomotive, minus its tender, a type the line never possessed, and the incorrect rendering of the Manx motto *Stabit quocunque jeceris* as *Concunque lecris stabit*. The transfer measures 6¼ in. in diameter and dates back to 1886.

The other railway on the island is the 3 ft. gauge Manx Electric, from Douglas along the coast to Ramsey, the final section of which was completed on 24th July 1899. Together with its 3 ft. 6 in. gauge appendage, the Snaefell Mountain Railway from Laxey, the total route mileage is 22.

A simple version of the national emblem was adopted as a device and this is reproduced on car vermilion. In an earlier variant the motto *Whichever way you throw me I stand* was shown *Quocunque jeceris stabit*. The overall size of the transfer is 10¾ in. wide × 13 in. high. It was preceded by a smaller and similar transfer 10½ in. wide × 10¾ in. high in which *jeceris* was spelt *iceeris*!

The Manx Electric Railway was transferred to the ownership of the Isle of Man Government on 1st June 1957.

Manx Electric 1st device
W. H. D. Faulkner Collection

Manx Electric 3rd device

Keighley & Worth Valley Light Railway

Authorised to build a line from the Leeds and Bradford extension of the Midland at Keighley to Haworth and Lowertown, the Keighley & Worth Valley Railway was incorporated in 1862. Its 4¾ miles of line, terminating at Oxenhope, were brought into use in 1867. It was worked by the Midland, vested in that company from 1st July 1881 and finally dissolved under the Midland Railway Act of 1886.

After closure of the line to passenger traffic in 1961 and to goods in the following year the old name would have remained in oblivion but for the formation of the Keighley & Worth Valley Preservation Society, the object of which was to resume the running of passenger trains. Eventually the Keighley & Worth Valley Light Railway Ltd, the directors of which were all officers of the society, negotiated a contract with British Railways under which, for an annual payment, control of the line was to be assumed, except for the last 100 yards into platform No 4 at Keighley station; these were to be leased. After much hard work, the first trains under the new order of things were operated on 29th June 1968 and the line at present offers steam hauled train services at weekends and bank holidays.

The simple emblem, worn chiefly by the locomotives, was produced by Butchers and is illustrated. The garter encircling the shield is red with gilt and black edging and ornamentation and black outlined white lettering.

Keighley & Worth Valley device

The shield is green, the blue *bordure embattled* being taken from the arms of Keighley. The three gilt coupled wheels *in chief* (which lack a crank pin on the middle one) denote the predominating wheel arrangement of the locomotives which worked the line when it was an ordinary branch. The two blue wavy bands on a white ground indicate the river Worth. And the gilt dragon's wing on a red and gilt wreath is taken from the LMS armorial device. Historically, a wyvern would have been more appropriate.

See Supplement p. 14

Listowel & Ballybunion Railway

Much nonsense has been aired about the advantages of the monorail and, during recent years, money has been wasted on consultants commissioned by the uninitiated to examine the extravagant claims of its protagonists. The hard truth is that the monorail is quite incapable of meeting the heavy demands a modern railway has to fulfil, whether passenger or freight or both. The fun fair and the exhibition ground are the elements to which it is best suited and should be restricted.

Key plate for Listowel & Ballybunion emblem
W. H. D. Faulkner Collection

In the 1880s a Frenchman named Lartigue invented one of the earliest systems. Locomotives and rolling stock of duplex construction and equipped centrally with wheels having double flanges rode a single rail elevated about 3 ft. 6 in. above ground by means of steel trestles. The latter carried guide rails either side, on which ran small transverse wheels fitted beneath each locomotive, carriage and wagon. Locomotives were suspended on three coupled axles, carriages and other vehicles on two axles.

Campbeltown & Macrihanish
BRB Collection

Lynton & Barnstaple
BRB Collection

North Wales·Narrow Gauge

PLATE 23

British Transport Commission coat of arms

Ulster Transport Authority coat of arms

PLATE 24

The Listowel & Ballybunion Railway was incorporated in 1886 to demonstrate the Lartigue system over 9¼ miles of monorail between the places in its title. It was opened on Leap Year's Day 1888 with some ceremony and began operations with 3 locomotives, 13 carriages and 11 freight vehicles all built in England.

An unusual emblem was produced by Tearnes, of which no transfer is known to have survived. But the 10¼ in. diameter key plate of it is, happily, still in existence and the first illustration of it ever to be published is reproduced. The pictorial part shows the end section of a coach, in which a running wheel and two guide wheels can be clearly seen.

Had the line been built near a large tourist centre such as Dublin or Cork its novelty might have attracted regular support from holidaymakers. But its remote location in County Kerry doomed it to failure and a Receiver was appointed as early as 1897. After an unsuccessful attempt had been made in 1924 to include it in the formation of the Great Southern Railways it was closed on 14th October of that year and the Receiver turned his attentions elsewhere.

Liverpool Overhead Railway

There was a time when one could enjoy a lightning tour of some six miles of fascinating dockland by taking a 28 minute trip on the Liverpool Overhead, which was the most important of the railways to escape nationalisation at the beginning of 1948.

The Liverpool Overhead was incorporated in 1888 and opened between Herculaneum Dock and Alexandra Dock on 6th March 1893. It was extended northwards from Alexandra Dock to Seaforth Sands on 30th April 1894 and southwards from Herculaneum Dock to Dingle on 21st December 1896. The total route mileage was 6½, all but three-quarters of a mile of which were elevated, mainly on girder structures.

Adopting electric traction at the outset, it was the first electrically operated elevated railway in the world. It was also the first in this country to have automatic signals, which made their *début* when the line was first opened, and when these were replaced by two-aspect colour light signals, operated by track circuit, in 1920, the latter were again the first of their kind in Great Britain.

The Liverpool Overhead adopted no armorial device, but contented itself with the extensive use of a monogram formed by its initials. This was to be seen on uniform buttons, on cap badges and, in colour, on the sides of the electric motor coaches and trailers, of which there were 38 and 19 respectively when the line was closed.

Varnished teak was the passenger rolling stock exterior finish until about 1948, when a two-colour livery consisting of a light brown upper half and a darker brown lower half, separated by a narrow red band, was adopted. The company's monogram, which is reproduced, was transferred centrally on each coach below the waist line. It measures $12\frac{3}{8}$ in. wide $\times$ 14 in. high over black shading, the garter having the usual gilt edging, ornamentation and lettering. The garter itself is red, shaded black, save for the short pendant piece, which is dark brown. Rather unusually, each letter in the monogram, the background of which is transparent, is coloured differently. The L is red, shaded white and black; the O is olive green, similarly shaded; the R is gilt, outlined black; and the C is golden yellow, again shaded white and black.

But despite the new livery and brightening up of stations, which included name signs rather similar to those on London's Underground, the line never seemed to recover from the heavy air raid damage it sustained during the last war. In 1956, when over £1½ millions were needed for structural repairs, there were no takers, and the company ceased to operate on 30th December. And Liverpool lost one of its most useful and interesting landmarks.

Liverpool Overhead Railway garter monogram

Lynton & Barnstaple Railway

Of all the narrow gauge railways in the British Isles the 1 ft. 11½ in.
Lynton & Barnstaple was undoubtedly one of the best loved. Its equipment
was far superior to most of its contemporaries and the scenery it traversed
was, and still is, superb. What a tragedy that fate was not a little kinder!
If the line could have managed to survive another fifteen years or so there
is little doubt that it would have been preserved and today would be doing
good business.

Sir George Newnes, of publishing fame, was one of the prime movers to
link Lynton with Barnstaple by rail. The company's Bill was given the
Royal Assent on 27th June 1895 and the line was opened to the public
on 11th May 1898. It began operations with a stock of 3 dark green
locomotives, 16 bogie passenger coaches having lake bodies with white
upper panels, and 18 freight vehicles, of which there were both four-
wheeled and bogie types. Vacuum brakes were fitted throughout and the
coaches were mounted on roller bearings.

The company's initials and armorial device adorned the coach sides.
Only one example of the latter appears to have survived and, fortunately,
it is preserved in the British Railways Board Collection. The two shields
embraced within the garter display a castle and a stag, denoting Barnstaple
and Exmoor respectively. It is, in fact, a copy of the company's seal,
save for the exclusion of one of the winged feet of Mercury above the
shields and the word *Company* in the title.

In 1923 the Lynton & Barnstaple was purchased by the Southern Railway
and various improvements were immediately carried out. But already the
effects of road competition had been felt and soon only holiday-makers
were its chief support. When the Southern announced its intention to
close the line a meeting in opposition was held in Barnstaple, to which
all the delegates from Lynton travelled by car! . . . The last trains ran
on 29th September 1935.

Mersey Railway

Liverpool once enjoyed a unique transport distinction in this country; it
could boast the only elevated city railway as well as an underground
railway. The former is now gone, as noted on an earlier page, but the
latter is thriving and will be extended within the next few years.

Originally the underground line was incorporated in 1866 as the
Mersey Pneumatic Railway Company. The *Pneumatic* in the title was
dropped in 1868 and the first section, from James Street station in
Liverpool and thence under the Mersey through Hamilton Square and

Central stations in Birkenhead to Green Lane station in Tranmere, was opened to the public on 1st February 1886. Extensions to Birkenhead Park (where an end-on junction was formed with the Wirral Railway), to Rock Ferry and to Liverpool (CLC) were opened in 1888, 1891 and 1892 respectively. Electrification of the whole system of $4\frac{3}{4}$ route miles was completed on 4th May 1903, two years before London's Inner Circle was similarly converted.

| Mersey Railway device | Mersey Railway gilt uniform button (26mm dia) |

Gilt uniform buttons and maroon externally finished rolling stock, which consisted of 24 motor coaches and 33 trailers, were ornamented with the company's emblem, which was in use for some years before electrification. This was, appropriately, a liver bird (a cormorant) holding a branch of seaweed called laver in its beak, which is part of the Liverpool City arms. The transfer displayed on the rolling stock has a diameter of $14\frac{1}{2}$ in. over black shading. The circlet is red, the gilt edging being lined black on each side, and the lettering is gilt, shaded black. The centre is transparent, but for the dark green area on which the gilt liver bird stands.

The Mersey Railway retained its separate identity until nationalisation in 1948, when it became part of the London Midland Region of British Railways.

Nidd Valley Light Railway

In June 1937 a whole village and a railway went under the auctioneer's hammer. They were the Pennine hamlet of Scar House, near Pateley Bridge in Yorkshire, and the Nidd Valley Light Railway, both of which owed their existence solely to the development of the Bradford Corporation reservoirs at Scar House and Angram.

The railway was built, owned and worked by the Bradford Corporation, having been sanctioned by an order granted by the Light Railway Commissioners in March 1904. Construction was started in the following July and the line formally opened on 11th September 1907. It extended from its own station at Pateley Bridge, where there was a connexion to the North Eastern, and thence via stations at Wath-in-Nidderdale and Ramsgill to Lofthouse-in-Nidderdale, a distance of 6 miles. This was the public section of the line over which passenger trains were operated. There was a further 7 miles of private railway up to Angram.

Two ex-Metropolitan 4-4-0T engines and ten 4-wheeled carriages bought from the Maryport & Carlisle and Metropolitan Railways formed the initial fleet, the few goods vehicles being obtained new. The livery of engines and coaches alike was the Metropolitan deep crimson lake, but with a darker shade of yellow lining.

Bradford arms for Nidd Valley locomotives

Nidd Valley nickel uniform button (15mm dia)

David Swan Collection

On each side tank of the locomotives was displayed a transfer of the rather unusual coat of arms of Bradford measuring 12 in. wide × 11½ in. high. The arms and crest were granted in 1847 and their similarity to those of the Yorkshire family of Bradford suggests that one was based on the other. The supporters, which were granted in 1907, connote the woollen industry. The motto *Labor omnia vincit* means *Labour overcomes all difficulties*.

Staff uniform buttons had a nickel finish and were embossed with the boar's head from the crest. An example is illustrated.

By 1929 local bus competition was so adversely affecting the railway that Bradford Corporation closed it to the public on the last day of that year. Trains still ran for the construction of Scar House reservoir, but when that was completed in 1936 and the village of over a thousand people was forsaken, the *raison d'etre* of the Nidd Valley Light Railway no longer existed.

North Wales Narrow Gauge Railways

Encouraged by the success the 1 ft. 11½ in. gauge Festiniog Railway enjoyed as a result of its introduction of steam traction and regular passenger services, the North Wales Narrow Gauge Railways Company was incorporated in 1872 to build two distinct lines of the same gauge, described prosaically as the General Undertaking and the Moel–Tryfan Undertaking.

The first of these, consisting of 23 miles of track from Bettws-y-Coed through Beddgelert to a junction with the Croesor & Portmadoc Railway, was abandoned in 1876 and never built. The second was for a line from Dinas, on the London & North Western, to Bryngwyn, and from Tryfan Junction, on this line, to Rhyd-ddu. It was opened in instalments, being completed with the section from Quellyn to Rhyd-ddu (later renamed South Snowdon) on 14th May 1881, and totalled some 11 route miles.

An attractive and now very rare armorial transfer was designed for display on the coaches of the railway. It consists of a rather riotous looking red Welsh dragon on a white shield, which is shaded grey and edged with gilt embellishments. The title of the company is in black letters on a white scroll shaded grey and is threaded through the gilt *decor* at the base, which has a red jewelled pendant. Overall it measures 8⅞ in. wide × 8¼ in. high.

A simpler and a not very original emblem was worn by some of the five crimson red locomotives and this, too, is illustrated. It is also very rare, dating back to 1875.

Under the Light Railways Acts of 1896 and 1912 the Welsh Highland

Railway was incorporated in 1922 to acquire, as from 1st January of that year, the NWNG and the Portmadoc, Beddgelert & South Snowdon (the former Croesor & Portmadoc) and to create a new through route by linking the two systems. This was achieved on 1st June 1923 when the 8¾ mile South Snowdon–Croesor Junction line was completed.

The Welsh Highland possessed no heraldic device and, unfortunately, was a financial failure from the start. A Receiver (the ubiquitous Lt. Col. H. F. Stephens) came on the scene in 1927 and, seven years later, after unsuccessful attempts had been made to persuade either the LMS or Great Western to take over the line, it was leased to the Festiniog Railway. But no better results were forthcoming and within three years the Festiniog had had enough. The last trains ran on 1st June 1937.

Subsequently Welsh Highland Light Railway (1963) Ltd was set up with the dual objects of restoring all or part of the line and of operating a service likely to be of use to tourists in the area.

North Wales Narrow Gauge locomotive device
BRB Collection

Romney, Hythe & Dymchurch Light Railway

Two erstwhile top-rank racing motorists, Captain J. E. P. Howey and Count Louis Zborowski, ardent miniature railway enthusiasts, conceived the 15 in. gauge line which eventually materialised as the Romney, Hythe & Dymchurch. Count Zborowski was killed whilst motor racing, before a suitable location had been found, and it fell to Captain Howey to bring the project to fruition.

Work was started in 1926 and, double track throughout, the railway was opened for traffic over 8¼ miles between Hythe and New Romney via Dymchurch in July 1927. A double track extension (single since the last war) from New Romney to Dungeness, 5½ miles, was completed during 1928–1929. The line was requisitioned by the Army in June 1940 and, after honourable and useful war service, was re-opened to the public in March 1946 to continue serving the several holiday camps and numerous summer visitors to the area.

A simple transfer emblem was devised for the passenger rolling stock. This takes the form of a red circlet of 5¼ in. diameter overall, edged in gilt and shaded black, carrying the title of the railway in black letters outlined in gilt. Within, a white scroll bears the apt motto *Multum in parvo—Much in Little*. It was designed by A. B. MacLeod, a British Railways chief officer now retired.

The Romney, Hythe & Dymchurch operates nine steam locomotives and a fleet of over sixty bogie coaches, most of which have roller bearings and are fully enclosed. *See Supplement p.14*

Romney, Hythe & Dymchurch device

Sutton Miniature Railway

The little 15 in. gauge railway which once wound its way for a mile through a picturesque wooded part of Sutton Park at Sutton Coldfield was one of the very few miniature lines to ornament its steam locomotives or rolling stock with a distinctive emblem transfer. Furthermore, it had two types made, one left hand and one right hand, *à la* British Railways.

These were not, however, displayed on the locomotives or their tenders but on the sides of the closed coaches, one at each end, facing inwards.

In this case the beast was a superior looking griffin, with wings *addorsed*, holding an Oxford blue shield lettered *SMR* in yellow and standing on a blue and gilt wreath. And well he might have an air of superiority, with his gilt hind parts and wings and red comb, feathers of two shades of green, tinted blue, and red talons! A gilt edged, ornamented and lettered Oxford blue garter formed the surround, giving the transfer a width of $4\frac{7}{8}$ in. and height of $5\frac{1}{2}$ in. It was designed by W. H. D. Faulkner.

The Sutton Miniature Railway was owned by the late T. Hunt, and his son W.T., of Hunt Bros (Oldbury) Ltd, Griffin Works (hence the griffin in the emblem) at Oldbury. It was brought into use during the first decade of this century and, after a busy life giving enjoyment to countless children and adults, was closed down in 1962. At its peak the line was operated with 4 steam locomotives, a petrol driven rail car and 10 bogie passenger carrying vehicles, all of the latter being provided with roller bearings.

Sutton Miniature Railway device

Talyllyn Railway

The success of steam traction on the Festiniog Railway encouraged the formation of the Talyllyn Railway, which was incorporated in 1865 for the construction of a line from the Bryn Eglwys quarries of the Aberdovey Slate Company to the Cambrian Railways at Towyn. The minimum gauge permitted by its Act, 2 ft. 3 in. was adopted. The line was opened for goods traffic in 1865 and for passengers in the following year over the $6\frac{1}{2}$ miles between Abergynolwyn and Towyn.

See
Supplement
p. 14

Work at the quarries ceased in 1947, and with the death in 1950 of the then owner of the line, Sir Henry Hadyn Jones, who had been determined to keep it open, the future looked ominous. But a group of enthusiasts thought otherwise, and the Talyllyn Railway Preservation Society was formed to raise the necessary finance. Arrangements were made with the existing shareholders whereby the company's shares were put into the hands of a new non-profit making company, whose directors were drawn from the Talyllyn Railway and from the new society. Unremitting efforts ever since have ensured the success of the enterprise.

No armorial device was displayed in the days of the original company, but in the middle 1950s a neat garter transfer, designed by W. H. D. Faulkner, made its appearance and is on locomotives and coaches in use. It measures 9 in. wide × 10¾ in. high over black shading. The Prince of Wales' feathers, in white shaded grey, held in a gilt crown with red and green jewels, together with the motto *Ich Dien* in gilt on Royal blue, edged gilt, form the centrepiece on a transparent background. The encircling garter is also of Royal blue edged and ornamented in gilt, with gilt *serif* letters outlined black.

The Royal cipher adorns the gilt uniform buttons of the staff, partly surrounded by the legend *Talyllyn Railway Company*.

Talyllyn device

Weston, Clevedon & Portishead Railway

This line was opened in 1897 as a standard gauge steam tramway between the Bristol Channel resorts of Weston-super-Mare and Clevedon, having been incorporated twelve years earlier. It became a light railway in 1899 and the extension from Clevedon to Portishead was brought into use in 1907, making the total route mileage 14½. Physical connexions were effected with the Great Western at Clevedon and Portishead.

During its lifetime the company indulged in a miscellany of secondhand locomotives and rolling stock. By far the most distinctive and uniform in appearance were the half-a-dozen bogie cars with clerestory roofs and end observation platforms which were bought new from the Lancaster Railway Carriage & Wagon Co Ltd in 1899. Crimson lake, lined black and vermilion, was originally the livery for both engines and carriages; later black was assumed for the former and brown for the latter, although green also made an appearance as a coach livery.

No armorial device was employed but the very Spartan garter illustrated was in use for some years. It measures 10 in. wide × 11 in. high and is something of a rarity. The garter is gilt, thinly edged red inside and out, and red is also the colour of the rather fragile looking lettering.

The Weston, Clevedon & Portishead was not one of those undertakings affected by the grouping nor did it come under the control of the Minister of Transport in September 1939. Largely because of war conditions the last passenger trains ran on 18th May 1940 and the line with unfortunate initials was abandoned.

Weston, Clevedon & Portishead garter

Severn Valley Rly
Snowdon Mountain Rly
Strathspey Rly

see Supplement p. 15

PART NINE

The National Systems

British Railways

The advent of the British Transport Commission, aided by the Railway, the Docks & Inland Waterways, the Road Transport, the London Transport and the Hotels Executives, heralded the brave new dawn of 1948. We are concerned here chiefly with the Railway Executive, which embraced some sixty railway undertakings and was by far and away the largest element in the nationalised set-up. It assumed *British Railways* as a collective title for the whole railway system, apart from the lines of London Transport. Its inheritance was 52,000 miles of track, including sidings, 20,000 locomotives, 45,000 passenger vehicles and 1,230,000 freight vehicles, in round figures.

Six provisional regions were made responsible to the Railway Executive, taking the place of the 'Big Four', namely Eastern (LNER Southern Area), North Eastern (LNER North Eastern Area), London Midland (LMS lines in England and Wales), Scottish (LMS and LNER lines in Scotland), Southern (SR) and Western (GWR). The LMS lines in Northern Ireland continued to be administered by the Northern Counties Committee and in 1949 were purchased by the recently formed Ulster Transport Authority.

Standard liveries for locomotives and rolling stock were not finalised until the early part of 1949 and were preceded by the assignment of regional colours for other purposes. The latter were: Eastern, Oxford blue; North Eastern, tangerine; London Midland, crimson lake; Scottish, Cambridge blue; Southern, middle green; and Western, light chocolate. As these colours were largely destined to be manifested in station and other signs, and hardly anywhere else, the decision was unfortunate in two directions. It did nothing to foster a much needed sense of unity, and it introduced at least two colours highly unsuitable for signs . . . drab chocolate and bilious tangerine.

245

On the credit side, Gill Sans lettering, which the LNER had exploited so successfully, was adopted for universal use. Soon it appeared on rail and road vehicles, signs of all kinds, timetables and letterpress posters. It was followed by a simple totem which, even if it did smack somewhat of London Transport (who, after all, were now in the same camp), acted as a distinctive symbol on posters, press advertisements and other publicity material, as a cap badge for uniformed staff, and as a lamp tablet for the display of station names. In a few years it had become instantly recognisable as the insignia of British Railways, even without the inclusion of the title.

The totem was extensively used in various types of vitreous enamel station fascia signs of the appropriate regional colour, sometimes purely as *décor*, when it was often shown in dumb form. Extensive station frontages, such as St Pancras and Manchester Central, were effectively marked by large neon totems. Internally illuminated mast signs, carrying the symbol and that of London Transport, were installed at stations between Queens Park and Watford, through which Bakerloo line trains operated over London Midland metals. A typical example is illustrated.

Some time after experiments on locomotives Nos 61001 and 61009 at Stratford in April 1948, British Railways saw fit to introduce another symbol, the exhibition of which was chiefly confined to the tender and tank sides of locomotives. It was a poor reflection of the British Transport Commission seal and could be described as a Wembley Exhibition 1924–1925 style lion, somewhat emaciated, astride a London Transport bar and circle, which had been converted into a spoked wheel, bearing the title *British Railways*. Butchers were the manufacturers and two transfers were made, one right-hand and the other left-hand, so that the lion could always face towards the leading end of the locomotive. Three sizes have been noted, the standard of 15 in. wide × 15½ in. high, a large version 26½ in. wide × 28 in. high and a small version 8½ in. wide × 9 in. high. The lion was chrome yellow, lined red, the wheel red and white and the title panel black and white. A modified design was used for the house flags of British Railways ships.

Altogether, its need was highly questionable. It evoked more derision than interest at a time when the railways were grappling with the twin problems of deferred maintenance arising from the recent war and the biggest organisational upheaval in their history. It was promptly, and deservedly, dubbed 'the ferret and dartboard' by the railway fraternity. Fortunately its life was a short one and nobody seemed to regret its demise.

In 1956 the British Transport Commission was granted an achievement by the King of Arms and the Lord Lyon of Scotland, so following in the footsteps of the Great Central, the LNER and the Southern. The striking design is illustrated and it will be noted that a pleasant salute to past

British Railways 1st emblem for general use

British Railways emblem for locomotives

Typical applications of British Railways and London
Transport emblems at a London suburban station

generations of railwaymen was given by embodying *Forward* as one of the mottoes; the other, *Velociter Securiter—Swift and sure*, was also an apt touch. The green field of the arms (shield) represents the open countryside. It is crossed by two pairs of narrow *barrulets* (diminutive of the bar) for the railways, between which is a *fess* (band) representing the roads, with two wavy bars superimposed thereon to denote the waterways. In the *chief* (top) of the arms the three wheels symbolise railway locomotives and rolling stock and in the base the chained portcullis indicates the ports and harbours of the undertaking. Regrettably, no transfer was made of this noteworthy coat of arms.

The crest of the device, which consists of a demi-lion *rampant*, holding between its paws a wheel similar to those in the arms, was adapted for the embellishment of locomotives (thereby displacing the first unsatisfactory emblem), motor coaches of electric and diesel multiple-unit stock and some main line coaches. Three versions were produced and are illustrated, two of them being transfers. In all three the basic design was the same; the demi-lion is *issuant* from an heraldic crown on which are arranged the English rose, the Scottish thistle, the Welsh leek and the oak to represent all Great Britain.

In the larger of the two transfers, which measures $30\frac{1}{4}$ in. wide $\times$ $14\frac{3}{4}$ in. high and was displayed on locomotives, the whole of the background is transparent, so that the body colour to which it is affixed is assumed. The lion is red, the wheel is silver and the crown, lettering and framing are buff, the two last named being outlined in black.

The smaller and purely circular transfer of $16\frac{1}{2}$ in. diameter, which was assigned to motor and main line stock, has a transparent outer band, the edging, lettering and ornamentation of which are buff, outlined in black. Within the band a red lion, silver wheel and buff crown are given a cream background.

With the electrification of the London Midland main line out of Euston to Liverpool and Manchester, the third and most handsome version was devised for the ornamentation of the sleek new electric locomotives. This was made of metal, having a chrome finish, and consisted simply of the lion, wheel and crown, the whole device measuring 18 in. wide $\times$ 18 in. high. The blue bodies of the locomotives made an excellent background. Electrification elsewhere had already produced another emblem, this time of local application. With the completion of the first stage of the Glasgow suburban electrification in 1961, covering 52 route miles on the north bank of the Clyde, a special symbol was devised for train departure sheets, station marker signs and general publicity. It consists of a blue V, on its side, facing right, across a yellow V, on its side, facing left, the whole being given a black background.

BTC crest for locomotives

BTC crest for coaches

Chrome finished metal BTC crest for electric locomotives

One more symbol of limited application followed in 1963. This was the freight service symbol reproduced, which was soon to be seen extensively on certain types of equipment, especially containers. But even on containers, with the words *door to door* in close proximity, the man-in-the-street mistook it, almost invariably, for a bi-directional arrow, not recognising the stylised container its designer obviously intended it to be. Psychologically, it was also a poor effort, appearing during a period when British Railways were under a prolonged heavy fire of public criticism and giving ammunition to those who complained that the railways did not know which way they were going. Historically, it heralded an era of 'arrowmania' which has yet to pass away.

There is an air of sterility today amongst those whose job it is to design industrial and commercial symbols. Most of them seem to be incapable of producing little more than some form of arrow, singly or two or three at a time. There are arrow symbols for railways (a particularly repulsive one is now the insignia of the Netherlands Railways), for buses, for road delivery vans, for two large industrial groups, for a television company, for a bank with numerous branches and, in the form of a debased Union Jack, for an airline. The current symbol of British Railways started a fashion which sooner rather than later is bound to become old hat because it is being flogged to death.

The symbol is one of the primary elements in a corporate identity programme which British Railways, now on its own since the British Transport Commission was dissolved at the end of 1962, introduced early in 1965 in its search for a new public image. Officially it is described as consisting of 'two-way traffic arrows on parallel lines representing tracks'. The top arrow therefore always points to the right (because the trains keep to the left), save only in the case of ships' funnels and ships' flags, where the top arrow will point forward on the port-side. It was conceived by Design Research Unit and, although it is by no means generally liked and has been aptly dubbed 'the barbed wire', it does represent an attempt to devise a distinctive, instantly recognisable symbol.

It is accompanied by a new form of lettering known as *Rail* alphabet, the noble Gill Sans being unceremoniously interred, and the logotype *British Rail* in the upper and lower case of the alphabet. These are the really questionable elements. Their protagonists would have one believe that the new alphabet is more legible than Gill and that the senseless emasculation *British Rail* is 'more forceful, simple to read and comprehend'. If this official blurb has a single grain of truth in it, then indeed the British have become a race of morons. In fact, both exemplify a case of change for the sake of change by people who were content to swallow the gimmicks served up by their consultants.

Glasgow electrification symbol
Photo: British Railways

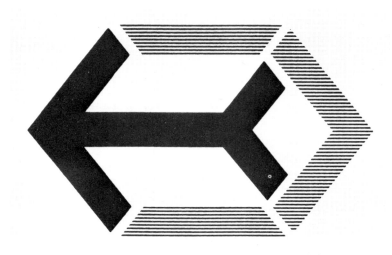

British Railways freight service symbol

The house colours of the programme—blue, grey and flame red—are its best feature. Hitherto there had been no real unity in the liveries of British Railways; now blue locomotives and blue or blue and grey coaches are to be seen everywhere. And slowly but surely the signs at stations are losing their regional colours for the more legible combination of black lettering on a white background, which should have been adopted at the very outset in 1948.

Chrome finished British Railways symbol now used for
electric locomotives

Coras Iompair Eireann

The Irish Transport Company—Coras Iompair Eireann, or CIE for short—was created on 1st January 1945 by the merging of the Dublin United Transport Co Ltd with the Great Southern Railways. The Grand Union Canal was added to CIE five years later and when that portion of the Great Northern Railway Board in Eire followed suit on 1st October 1958 all public railway services in the republic were in the hands of CIE.

Irish railways have always shown a partiality for heraldic *décor*, as earlier pages have demonstrated, and it was therefore rather surprising that CIE did not provide itself with an armorial device. Instead, a prosaic winged wheel emblem, which had been originally introduced by Dublin United Transport, was adopted. Grass green, gilt outlined transfers, of two or three sizes, were made, the standard being of 33 in. extreme overall width × 14⅜ in. high. Reverse transfers were also produced.

It was displayed on the green passenger locomotives and coaching stock (the latter were finished in two shades, as were some diesel locomotives) and on buses and other road vehicles, a reverse transfer being used on the offside of the last named. On railway wagons it was painted on in white. As a cap badge it was finished in nickel silver. It did not appear to enjoy much popularity and was soon called the 'flying snail'.

CIE first symbol

CIE current symbol

At the end of 1963, on the advice of Scandinavian industrial consultants, CIE effected a complete change of livery which embraced the adoption of the colours white, dawn grey, dark blue, black and ochre-orange. All rolling stock, rail and road, was to be painted eventually in combinations of these colours. At the same time a new universal symbol was introduced; this was not in the usual transfer form, being made of self-adhesive plastic with a peel-off backing.

The ochre-orange version of the symbol is reproduced. This has a diameter of $7\frac{7}{8}$ in., the black letters inside having a depth of $2\frac{5}{8}$ in., and the usual colours against which it is displayed are black, dark blue and dawn grey. The similar coaching stock version, which is applied to an ochre-orange background, has black segments edged with a gold line.

It is an improvement on its predecessor in that it is somewhat more original in design, but it has not escaped the wit of the Irish, amongst whom it is often referred to as the 'broken wheel', the reward a well-meaning Board gets for its efforts!

Ulster Transport Authority

The Transport Act (Northern Ireland) of 1948 created the Ulster Transport Authority, which began to function on 1st October of that year. Vested in it were the Belfast & County Down Railway, with its hotels undertaking, and the passenger and freight road services of the Northern Ireland Road Transport Board. The latter had been formed in 1935 to take over very nearly all public passenger and goods road motor concerns in Northern Ireland, including those of the Great Northern, the LMS (Northern Counties Committee) and the Belfast & County Down Railways.

On 1st April 1949 the Northern Counties Railway and its hotels were vested in the UTA, having been purchased from the British Transport Commission. The Northern Ireland portion of the Great Northern Railway Board was acquired on 1st October 1958.

The UTA adopted the Red Hand of Ulster on a silver shield as its emblem. In transfer form, for application to locomotives, diesel rail cars and coaches, it was enclosed in a circlet bearing the legend *Ulster*

UTA device

NIR monogram on York Road station
Photo: Northern Ireland Railways

NIR monogram on coach
Photo: Northern Ireland Railways

255

Transport; the whole frame is coloured a deep buff, lined red, and measures 14 in. in diameter.

In 1960 the UTA gave itself the distinction of a full achievement, granted by Letters Patent from the College of Arms. At the time of writing it is the last of its kind and it provides a colourful, refreshing note with which to end these pages. Two sizes, 10¼ in. wide × 12 in. high and 6⅞ in. wide × 8 in. high, were printed.

The green shield symbolises Northern Ireland and the *bend* across it a road or a railway. The six counties are denoted by the coronets, as an earl traditionally ruled a county. A gold flying horse, *rampant* on a green and gold wreath, and charged on the shoulder with a red *dexter* hand, palm outwards, makes an appropriate crest. The supporters, a red lion and an Irish elk in natural colours, symbolise the connexions with the United Kingdom and Ireland, the mural crowns around their necks representing the boroughs of Belfast and Derry. And what better translation of the motto *Transportatio cultum significat* could one suggest than *Transportation is civilisation*?

By way of postscript it must be recorded that the UTA was reorganised in 1967 to keep up with the political Joneses across the Irish Sea. Its railway, road passenger and road freight sections were hived off into separate units, as a consequence of which Northern Ireland Railways Company Ltd was incorporated on 21st April of that year. NIR did not, however, begin to function officially until 1st April 1968, when it marked the occasion, and the completion of improvements at York Road station, Belfast, with the unveiling of its symbol on the front of the building by the Minister for Development. The new symbol took the position formerly occupied by the UTA coat of arms and can hardly be said to rank amongst the improvements carried out.

Perhaps one day an industrial consultant will come along and pick up some easy money by suggesting something only marginally better.

And perhaps one day there will be the usual swing of the pendulum, and heraldry, which has been a part of our heritage for over 700 years, will once again be regarded as appropriate for the railways of the country which gave railways to the world.

Acknowledgements

For the preparation of this book I have had the benefit of documentary information supplied by W. H. D. Faulkner and throughout its compilation I have enjoyed his encouragement and assistance. The resources of the BRB Archivist, E. H. Fowkes, and of the BRB Curator of Historical Relics, J. H. Scholes, have always been available to me and I would thank them both, and their staff, for help freely given whenever sought. For the loan of most of the vintage uniform buttons my grateful thanks are due to David Swan. Likewise I am indebted to Michael Robbins for some hitherto unpublished information about London Transport devices.

To R. E. Vincent I record my appreciation for some three-quarters of the colour photography from which the colour plates have been made. The remainder of this work was carried out by my son Andrew, to whom credit is also due for all black and white photography, unless stated otherwise. Most of the devices are from my own collection, but where this is not so the owner is indicated.

As in the case of earlier books of mine I have again been helped by my wife with the typing and checking and with valuable constructive criticism. Others to whom my thanks are due for information or illustrative material are :

Michael Andress
D. J. W. Brough
Gerald Cattell
R. N. Clements
T. Cott
Alan Dixon
Professor C. J. Fordyce
P. J. Garland
Gerald Hartley
W. T. Hunt
M. G. Joly

E. R. Lacey
D. C. McKelvey
G. R. Mahon
G. H. Mapleston
John Marshall
K. A. Murray
T. Noble
Rupert Powell
F. B. Stitt
P. Sunderland
L. Ward

together with H. Waring, Managing Director of Northern Ireland Railways; G. P. O'Shea, Architect of Coras Iompair Eireann; Noel Macdonald, General Manager of Sheffield Transport; R. Shaw, Traffic Superintendent of Glasgow Corporation Transport; H. W. E. Butcher, Managing Director of J. H. Butcher & Co Ltd; David C. Young of City of Norwich Museums; the Chief Herald of Dublin Castle; the Deputy Librarian of the City of London Guildhall Library; the Chief Librarians of the Boroughs of Derby and Huddersfield; and the Town Clerks of Bideford, Birkenhead and Campbeltown.

Bibliography

Book of Public Arms by A. C. Fox-Davies (1915)
Bradshaw's Railway Manual, Shareholders' Guide & Directory
Civic Heraldry by C. W. Scott-Giles
General Armory by Sir Bernard Burke, CB LLD Ulster King of Arms (1884)
Intelligible Heraldry by C. & A. Lynch-Robinson (1948)
Journal of the Irish Railway Record Society
Railway Magazine
Railway World
Universal Directory of Railway Officials & Railway Year Book

Index

Black and white illustrations indicated by **bold** type

Supplement to
RAILWAY HERALDRY
Published by the Author

Since my long-out-of-print *Railway Heraldry* appeared in 1973, important information about old designs has come to light, some hitherto unrecorded designs have been discovered and a few interesting new ones have been introduced.

The publishers were unwilling to print a new and enlarged edition, so I decided to publish the additional material myself, in the form of this illustrated supplement, for all those who own a copy of my book and any others who may be interested. It also contains corrections of a few typographical and other errors in *Railway Heraldry*.

I record with pleasure my thanks to the owners of the various collections acknowledged and to those who provided photographs and information.

Copies of this supplement, £1.50 prepaid, post free, are obtainable only from me at Wyverns, Audlem, Cheshire CW3 0AL.

August 1985   George Dow

Printed by Johnsons of Nantwich Ltd.

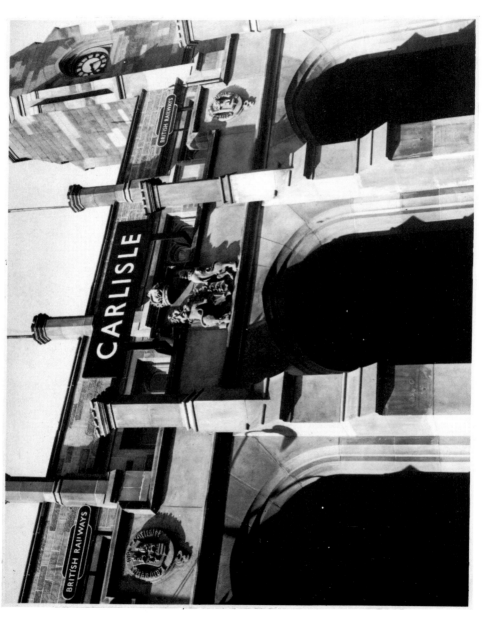

The old and not so new. The arcaded entrance to Sir William Tite's Victorian-Tudor Carlisle Citadel station. It embodies stone representations of the Royal arms (centre) and heraldic emblems of the Lancaster & Carlisle Railway (left) and Caledonian Railway (right). They are surmounted by British Railways totems and station name in crimson lake vitreous enamel lettered in white. C'll at b t e ital*d*

Page 13 Caledonian Railway

The earliest emblem employed by this railway appears to have consisted of the Scottish lion and thistle, exemplified by this 24mm diameter nickel uniform button in the Collection of D. P. Van Court of Madison, New Jersey, U.S.A. The device, minus the thistle, is also to be seen in the 1956 photograph of the entrance of Citadel station, Carlisle, reproduced opposite.

Page 16 Furness Railway

An unfortunate error in the text was made by the printer, after proof reading. Line 9 should read 'It contrasted strongly with the livery of ultramarine blue, with white'.

An unusual carved wood example of the Furness Railway coat of arms, once to be seen in the company's Board Room at Barrow-in-Furness and now preserved in the Gerald Hartley Collection, is illustrated. It is painted in the heraldic colours and measures 21in. wide x 26in. high.

Page 21 Highland Railway

Another early uniform button from the Van Court Collection and probably the first design of the Highland because it features the arms of Inverness and Aberdeen, inherited from a predecessor, the Inverness & Aberdeen Junction Railway. The button is of brass and has a diameter of 23.5mm.

Page 23 Lancashire & Yorkshire Railway

An early uniform button of nickel, 26mm in diameter, from the J.H. Lucking Collection, unusual in that it includes the year of the company's incorporation. The Lancashire & Yorkshire began in 1836 as the Manchester & Leeds, the change of name taking place eleven years later.

Page 32 London & North Western Railway

A cast iron version of the London & North Western device was once to be seen among the roof trusses of Leeds New station, which was owned jointly with the North Eastern. All the components are included, Britannia with her trident, shield and lion, and the multi-arched viaduct with its train, but none is in its customary position! The example illustrated is preserved in the Gerald Hartley Collection.

Page 40 Midland Railway

The first armorially embellished uniform buttons of the Midland Railway embodied the arms of five principal places it served, not six as in subsequent designs. The towns represented on this early 22mm diameter silver-plated button in the J.H. Lucking Collection are Leicester (top left), Derby (top centre), Nottingham (top right), Birmingham (bottom left) and Leeds (bottom right).

A circular form of its coat of arms was sometimes used by the Midland in publications and, in colour, at outdoor events at which it was represented, such as agricultural shows. This example, in the Gerald Hartley Collection, contains the arms of Birmingham, Derby and Bristol (left to right, top row) and Leicester, Lincoln and Leeds (left to right, bottom row). Supporters are the dolphin (left) and salamander (right) and the whole is surmounted by the wyvern as the crest.

Page 61 London, Midland & Scottish Railway

It has been discovered that there was yet another variation in the lining and lettering colours of the LMS 14⅛in diameter armorial transfer. In 1937 a silver lined and lettered version was introduced for the blue and silver coaches of the *Coronation Scot* express. The last paragraph on page 61 should, therefore, be amended to read: 'In thrice altering the lining and lettering colours of its armorial transfer to meet changes in livery the LMS was alone amongst British railway companies'.

Page **63** Great Central Railway

This gilt 28mm uniform button of the Sheffield, Ashton-under-Lyne & Manchester Railway from the J.H. Lucking Collection is a great rarity. The three shields represent the places in the company's title and are set beneath the heraldic rose of Lancashire.

Page **73** Great Eastern Railway

In lines 26-30 it is incorrectly stated that this company's metals did not reach the county of Northampton, the nearest point being Peterborough. B.S. Cooper of Amersham has drawn attention to the fact that in 1862 Peterborough was in Northamptonshire and so remained until the passage of the Local Government Act of 1888, which formed the separate administrative Soke of Peterborough out of part of the county of Northampton.

Page **79** North British Railway

An example of the circular 10in diameter North British Railway coat of arms transfer, from the Gerald Hartley Collection, is illustrated, together with a 23mm diameter brass finished marine department armorial uniform button from the Van Court Collection.

Page 81 North Eastern Railway

The ancient Great North of England Railway, which was an early predecessor of the North Eastern, not only adorned its coaches with the arms of York, Newcastle and Durham but also the brassards worn by its passenger train guards. The two styles traced are shown in these National Railway Museum photo-

graphs. Both have a black background, with gold lettering and ornamentation and the heraldic colours are the same, namely: York (left) white ground, red cross and gold lions; Newcastle (centre) red ground, gold castles; and Durham (right) blue ground, gold cross. The motto, *Per terras per flumina, By land and river,* is displayed on a purple ground in the case of guard No. 4 and a red ground in that of No. 18, the latter's legend at the base being in black characters on a gold panel.

At Leeds New station, the LNWR cast iron device described earlier in this supplement was matched by a cast iron version of the North Eastern coat of arms. The example shown below is in the Gerald Hartley Collection.

Page 93 Colne Valley & Halstead Railway

In line 25 'Nuremberg' is misspelled.

Page 104 Mid-Wales Railway

M.B. Spalding of Mawgan Porth has commented that the *motif* of this company's device is virtually a copy of Benedetto Pistrucci's renowned work for the British coinage, notably the sovereign. That was in those far-off days when our coinage was dignified, beautiful and of logical design. Pistrucci was chief designer and engraver at the Royal Mint from 1815.

Page 108 Rhymney Railway

This striking brass replica of the Rhymney Railway coat of arms was made from a drawing of 1901 by Daniel Meredith, the company's Chief Draughtsman. It is $9\frac{1}{2}$in square and was once to be seen in the General Manager's office at Caerphilly. It is now preserved in the Gerald Hartley Collection.

Also reproduced is the Rhymney Railway monogram which was displayed on coaches. Author's Collection.

9

Page 111 Burry Port & Gwendreath Valley Railway

An interesting example of internal heraldic *décor* is this emblem of the Burry Port & Gwendreath Valley Railway. At the base is the year of its incorporation and within are pictures denoting the company's marine and railway activities, with an escutcheon bearing the Prince of Wales' feathers superimposed. It is embossed on the cover of a free pass in the Edward Higgs Collection.

Page 111 Neath & Brecon Railway

Another rare example of internal heraldic *décor* is the heading taken from the stationery of the Neath & Brecon Railway General Manager and dating back to 1893. It embraces the arms of Neath (castle) and Brecon (robe), with a 2-2-2T locomotive above and, beneath, the motto *Perviam rectam,* which can be liberally translated as *Along the right lines.* From the Collection of D.T.H. Price.

Page 128 London & South Western Railway

In line 2 the locomotive stock should be shown as 912.

Page 146 City & South London Railway

I.D. Blee of London Transport has pointed out that a device rather similar to that illustrated in *Railway Heraldry* was embossed in gold on the cover of the City & South London Railway Rule Book of 1907.

Page 150 Metropolitan District Railway

In line 14 'predilection' is misspelled.

Page 174 Preston & Wyre Railway

Before this little railway was taken over jointly by the Lancashire & York-shire and London & North Western Railways in 1849 it made use of the arms of Sir Peter Hesketh Fleetwood on uniform buttons. Sir Peter, who founded Fleetwood at the mouth of the river Wyre, also financed the building of the railway from that place to Preston. His arms are shown on the accompanying 15mm diameter silver-plated uniform button in the Van Court Collection. Its description in heraldic language is 'Per pale nebuly azure and or, six martlets counter-changed, a canton argent.'

Page 174 Manchester South Junction & Altrincham Railway

The final design of armorial transfer for this jointly-owned railway had a green garter to harmonise with the Brunswick green external livery of the electric cars.

Page 176 Midland & Great Northern Joint Railway

In line 12 the year should be shown as 1858.

Page 190 Cork Bandon & South Coast Railway

In line 1 'of' should read 'on'.

Page 197 Tralee & Dingle Light Railway

The Author rashly observed that this narrow gauge railway never indulged in an armorial device. A design, based upon the seal, has since been discovered and is illustrated. It is in the form of a transfer measuring 8in wide x 9½in high,

mounted on a dark maroon shield, but in what way it was used is not yet known. The castle and crown are taken from the Tralee coat of arms, the castle (white with black doors and windows) being that of Tralee and the crown (gold with coloured jewels) representing King John, from whom Tralee is reputed to have obtained a charter in the late 1100s. The riband and pendant shamrock leaves are of gold, the former carrying in black Gaelic characters the legend 'The Iron Road of Tralee & Dingle', the only known Irish language inscription in railway nomenclature prior to 1924. This rare device is preserved in the Gerald Hartley Collection.

A guide published by the company in 1910-12, a copy of which was owned for many years by John Hegarty and is now in the Walter McGrath Collection of Cork, carried the device on its coloured 5½in by 4in front cover and is reproduced below.

Page 212 Railways in the Channel Islands

The Jersey Eastern used the simple emblem opposite on the covers of its free passes, this example being from the Edward Higgs Collection. The shield carries the three lions of Jersey and a representation of Gorey Castle, which the line reached from St. Helier. Photograph by David J. Froggatt.

Page 227 Railways in the Isle of Man

Fourth and fifth variations of the Isle of Man Railway device are shown. The first of these, produced in the form of a waterslide transfer, carries a green locomotive. The other, a more recent design, carries a red locomotive and an electric tram and trailer to denote the Manx Electric Railway. Appropriately the legend on the garter has been changed to read 'Isle of Man Railways'. Both are from the Gerald Hartley Collection.

Page 230 Keighley & Worth Valley Light Railway

A revised armorial emblem has been introduced by this preserved line and is shown in the accompanying photograph of one of its coloured car stickers. The garter and its fittings, which have yellow borders edged black, and the background to the shield, are cream coloured, the lettering being red. The shield is also red, with blue *bordure embattled,* and carries three heraldic Yorkshire roses, two blue and three white wavy bands to denote the river Worth and a yellow wyvern to represent the Midland Railway, the original operator and eventual owner of the line.

Page 239 Romney, Hythe & Dymchurch Light Railway

Soon after the publication of *Railway Heraldry* this railway produced an entirely new heraldic emblem for its passenger rolling stock. It took the form of the transparency illustrated. Measurements overall are $7\frac{3}{4}$in wide by $10\frac{3}{8}$in high. The garter is dark blue lined light blue, with white lettering, the clasp and buckle being yellow. The retained motto *Multum in parvo* is also in yellow, lined brown. The wheel is green, with yellow panels lined brown on its spokes, set on a gilt background and outlined in white, black and gilt. The white horse of Kent has a brown mane, tail and hooves. The whole design is outlined in gilt. Photograph by Andrew Dow.

Page 242 Talyllyn Railway

In line 2 'Haydn' is misspelled.

New entries

Three more heraldic devices have to be recorded, all of which, had it been possible, would have been included in part 8 of *Railway Heraldry*. They are:

Severn Valley Railway

The attractive armorial emblem introduced by this preserved line is usually to be seen in black and white in the house magazine and on postcards; it is available for members as a coloured metal badge; and, again in colour, as a car sticker, reproduced in the photograph.

In the design are represented two of the towns on the line, Bewdley (left) and Bridgnorth (right), separated by a wavy line to denote the river Severn. In both coloured versions Bewdley's anchor is shown in gilt on a white ground; the metal badge displays the castle of Bridgnorth in gilt on a pale blue ground, standing on a green sward, but in the car sticker the castle depicted in blue outline, is given a blue flecked ground and stands on a red sward. In both coloured versions the Severn is blue, edged gilt, and the encircling garter is red, lettered and edged gilt. Author's Collection.

Snowdon Mountain Railway

This appropriate transfer, measuring $12\frac{3}{8}$in by $12\frac{3}{8}$in overall, is displayed on carriages. Around and inside the cog wheel and around the rackrail is a green background. The cog wheel and rackrail are black, with white lettering. The Welsh dragon is red. Gerald Hartley Collection.

Strathspey Railway

It is good to be able to conclude these notes with the distinctive coat of arms of the Strathspey Railway because it was properly authorised in 1980 by Lord Lyon, King of Arms. The picture of it is taken from the colour plate reproduced in the Summer 1980 issue of the *Strathspey Express,* in which the hope was expressed that it will not be too long before the device appears on the locomotives and coaches of the company.

The components are a silver osprey on a blue ground (top left) to denote the Spey Valley; two gilt crowns on a red ground representing Clan Grant and hence the territory traversed by the railway (top right); and a locomotive wheel, black outlined in blue, supported by the red paws of the Scottish lion, the whole of the ground being gilt. The base is green, traversed by a wavy blue line edged black on a white ground to indicate the river Spey. The three main parts of the shield are edged black, as is the shield itself. The motto is Gaelic for 'Reborn', shown in black letters on a white riband edged black, the reverse side of which is red.